It's All
Connected

It's All Connected

An interactive leadership and healing journey
through the chakras

BY
Jessica Boots

Book cover by Jenna Zakrajsek
Yoga images: ©springhillyogadesign
Back photo by Hannah Franco

First edition 2025

ISBN 979-8-9986582-0-4

For Gabrielle.

My heart outside of my body.

My personal reminder that we all are connected.

My wise teacher who keeps me in the process of evolution.

"Be truly whole. And all things will return to you."

~Lao Tzu

Table of Contents

Each chapter contains a meditation script and a yoga flow. To make this more accessible for you, no matter where you are on your journey, I've uploaded a recording of each meditation script and each yoga practice. Use the QR code or link below to access those recordings.

https://www.leadandbewell.com/its-all-connected-resources

Introduction

"Isvara is the Sanskrit word for pure awareness, and is represented by the sound of OM, the universal vibration that connects us all."

– Patanjali

Why I Wrote This Book

Dear Reader,

I wrote this book to help you heal and evolve. I have lovingly filled it with my heart, my stories, information, tools and practices that have helped me heal and grow into the leader I am today.

Healing isn't linear, and it's never finished.

Healing is an inevitable part of growth, and as we grow as leaders, our healing is required.

Sometimes this healing occurs in small moments - like taking a mini digital fast from consuming too much social media - and other times healing is like an excavation - digging into the deepest parts of your soul and remembering your worth, your value and your purpose.

It is my prayer that this book supports your daily and ongoing growth so that you evolve with ease into the leader you already are at your core, and the world needs you to be.

This book is not meant to be read in one sitting. I invite you to think of it more like a conversation. We'll take time to listen to each other, learn from each other, with time to process in between.

I hope this book finds its way into your daily rhythms. Coming with you to local coffee shops and nature walks, so you can pause and reflect and seek inspiration both from its pages and your own lived experiences.

Like all of my favorite books, I hope it gets a little worn at the edges. Well loved. My mother used to say we had "loved off" the fuzz on our stuffed animals, and I hope that happens to this book. I hope the pages are a little tear stained, dog eared, highlighted, written in. A glimpse of external evidence of your internal growth.

Above all, I pray you feel my love. That was my mantra while writing to you.

Go deep Jess, write with love.

So I did. I hope you enjoy.

— Jess

How to Use This Book:

Throughout our time together, I hope you explore the parts of the book that speak to you. Your intuition will give you nudges and insights into the aspects that you are ready for. Listen. Follow. Then I hope you revisit it some other time, and hit repeat, and get curious to see if your intuition is ready for something new.

We are constantly evolving, and my prayer is that this book evolves with you. I hope it moves you, challenges you, breaks some old ways of thinking, and gives you permission to shed some unnecessary layers.

I will do my best to share honestly in a way that is in service to your evolution. This book is for you. It's not all about me. But I'm learning that it's always both. When I step into my story, when I give myself permission to be real and vulnerable and let myself shine, it's a gift to the world. It gives you the reminder that you too can take up as much space as you need, that your light deserves to shine bright as well.

There is an intentional order to how I structured the book. We start at the beginning. With our intentions, our prayers. We then work our way through the densest and most tangible of layers - earth, our roots - our purpose - and work our way up through the lightest, most ethereal - our connection to everything.

It is likely you will get stuck somewhere. That's ok. Listen to your body, your needs. The first three chapters are the most challenging in terms of unearthing things for us to work through. But they are the most essential. We're setting the foundation. It's ok to take the time. It's ok to take *your* time. I'll tell you right now, there is NO RUSH.

There are no bonus points for finishing this book in any amount of time. You are right on time.

In each chapter, I'll share some information, tell you some stories, offer practical ways to engage with the theme. Along the way, I'll extend many invitations. These exercises, reflections and explorations are ways for you to deepen your understanding of this leadership theme. Give yourself permission to let your growth take it's own journey.

Learning sometimes happens quickly, like a light switch turning on - we are flooded with understanding and deeply changed. Other times learning takes some time. We practice embodying certain mindsets, practices or habits, and we notice after weeks and months that something has shifted inside - like the night sky during the summer...the stars emerging one at a time until the view above you takes your breath away.

You might try every exploration, you might just try one. You might reach a further chapter, then realize you want to go back and revisit a previous one. Again, trust your intuition. Listen. Follow. Trust that you're doing it right.

If I may insist on something, I insist that you write. Or speak to someone. We make meaning through writing and speaking because it's too much to keep inside. Let it out. Let yourself make meaning. It doesn't need to be polished or perfect, just honest.

Why the Title: *It's All Connected*

The title for this book was so easy for me to choose. I thought it would be one of the last things to present itself in this whole book writing process, but no. It was one of the first.

I've said this phrase a million times, because our healing and our leadership are connected. Because when we have something going on at home, it impacts how we show up at work. When we injure a toe, we feel it in our shoulders. The number of times I listen to a client, or to myself, talk about things that are present in our lives - situations we are working through...and there's this moment of "well, of course. It's all connected. It makes sense that you feel this way."

My regular yoga practice really took off as a balance to all the running I was doing. I figured that stretching with more intention would help me be a better runner, and not have so much stiffness in the body. I was right. But, what I didn't anticipate was that I would uncover a pathway for healing so much more than my physical body. I experienced the interconnectedness of the mind and body and heart, and was fascinated by how sensations in my legs and hips could relate to how I understood the instability of my earliest childhood and how I showed in relationships as an adult. *Wasn't I just stretching my hamstrings?*

This first glimpse into how the body stores information, as well as the effect of deep breathing on our parasympathetic nervous system, just clicked for me. Of course stress in one area of our lives is going to pour over into other areas. Of course slowing down to heal one part of our hearts is going to trickle down and heal other parts of us as well. Of course when we heal the body, we heal the mind, and when we heal the mind, we heal the body. Of course, love and our hearts are at the center of it all.

I love learning the science behind the ancient practices, but I've also learned to trust in the mystery and the felt-sense experience. I felt calmer after I practiced yoga. I didn't necessarily need to know exactly what was happening on a hormonal level to know I wanted more.

I have learned about why yoga is so beneficial through the work of so many brilliant teachers, and one aspect I want to share here is the fascia. One of these teachers, Harvey Deutsch, a physical therapist and yoga teacher, shared so much wisdom about the fascia! This could be an entire other book in and of itself, but I'll be brief. Fascia is the connective tissue - some of which includes the tendons and ligaments- that wraps the entire body like shrink wrap. This fascia has many layers that wrap around and through the body. It can bunch up or get congested in some areas and we experience it as tension. For example, if I have soreness in one hip, I may have sensation in the opposite shoulder based on how I'm walking or compensating for the original sensation. *Connections, right?*

We feel best when the fascia is hydrated and supple. The muscles and bones can move with greater ease. When we practice yoga and deep breathing, we warm the body from the inside out, allowing tension in the fascia to release, which then gives way for the muscles to tone and stretch, and the skeleton of the body to move about the world with more freedom.

Still with me? Maybe take a moment and move your body - notice where you feel things connecting in unique and beautiful ways. Experience is a powerful teacher.

In Gabby's earliest months, which overlapped with the pandemic, I dove in deep to learning about the fascia and our interconnectedness. I practiced online with Seane Corn almost daily. I was so grateful to have access to one of my favorite teachers in a way I normally would not have. The necessity of having life online created connection in an otherwise increasingly disconnected world. The dichotomy of being isolated at home with a newborn, but participating in an ancient practice with others from around the world was really beautiful.

Seane teaches a lot about the fascia as well, and how trauma is stored in the body - often in this connective tissue. When we experience trauma, the body reacts. It goes into fight or flight, and it contracts, or tightens. As the muscles and connective tissue contract, the associated event gets stored in these areas as well. You know that feeling? When someone scares you and your whole body responds and tightens? It feels like self protection. Which, put simply, is what's happening. We're almost holding ourselves together, putting up armor, guarding our hearts and bodies from danger. It's necessary at the moment.

What happens though, is we keep that energy stored. We stay armored. We layer up. That self protection that was once needed, just stays with us, keeping us separate and contracted instead of open and available.

Yoga helps us heal.

Practicing mindful breathing and thoughtful poses allows time and heat to begin to soften the contracted tissues in the body, and the memories associated with them to be released.

So here I was, using my daughter's naptime to heal past versions of myself as they rose to the surface while I held lizard pose longer than most humans want to. It was again this reminder that *it's all connected.* The tension that was being released from my psoas muscle was both because I love to run, but also connected to the fear, guilt and shame I experienced as a child and young adult living life, and later as a woman trying to conceive. The tears that escaped after five rounds of upward facing bow pose were maybe from the exhaustion of a rigorous practice, but more clearly connected to the unresolved grief of pregnancy losses.

I was experiencing healing on a molecular level, a spiritual level, an emotional level and an energetic level. In yoga, we call these layers the koshas. There are five of these layers, or "sheaths". Seane Corn describes each of the five koshas in her book, *Revolution of the Soul.*[1] I'm summarizing here to give a sense of these layers, or koshas. The outer most layer is the Annamaya Kosha (the physical or food body), which is ultimately our container, our home, the gateway in. Underneath it is the Pranamaya Kosha, (the energy body), where our Prana or life force is flowing through the subtle body. It includes the breath, but it's so much more than that. This is where "the prana is charging up through the chakra system, opening up all the channels."[2] The framework for this book is in this layer - the subtle energy layer that we access when we get into our bodies, use our life force with intention, breathe deeply and with purpose, and get curious about what connections are possible.

Beneath the energy body is the Manomaya Kosha (the mental body), where the spinal cord and brain send messages throughout and to the body. At the mental body we see the clear connection between the mind and the body. Moving deeper still, the Vijnanamaya Kosha (the wisdom body) is where inner wisdom resides. So many of the energetic centers of the body we will visit in this book will connect to this layer - where deep trust, self knowing, and intuition reside. Finally, the Anandamaya Kosha (the bliss body) is the innermost layer, the quiet, peaceful place inside ourselves where we remember our connection to all things.

The knowledge of these layers, in addition to my expertise as an educator, is why I've designed each chapter to be experienced in so many different ways. There are opportunities to dive in intellectually - in your mind through learning information. I've shared stories so that you can connect to your heart and your emotions and what that brings up for you. I've offered practices to help you get into your body so that the history that lives in your cells can make its way to the surface. I've invited you to write so that you are not just receiving, but you are engaging with and embodying the material.

Choose your doorway in - they all lead to the same place, because, as you know by now, it's all connected.

Scope of Information

The information I share in this book is based on years of experience, learning, reading, practicing, formal and self study. I am so grateful for the list of experts I have listed in the resource section of this book. The teachers who have come before me, who have written their books, taught their classes, offered their gifts and shared their interpretation of the ancient texts, and the modern lived experience.

This book is not a comprehensive book on the chakras - if you're interested in that, please read *Eastern Body, Western Mind* or *The Wheels of Life*, both by Anodea Judith.

This book is not a textbook on all the yoga poses and philosophy - if that is peaking your interest, please seek out the brilliance of Janet Stone, Seane Corn, and countless others. The books are endless, but it helps to start from the foundation (*The Yoga Sutras, The Yamas and The Niyamas*).

This book is inspired by the healing, growth and learning that I have found as I used yoga as a method for evolving as a leader. The key concepts I'm referencing here are just the tip of the iceberg, and I encourage you to notice when you feel your curiosity lighting up and follow the threads.

One essential concept I will offer here is Kriya Yoga. In *The Path of The Yoga Sutras, a practical guide to the core of yoga*, Nicolai Bachman writes, "Kriya Yoga, defined by Pantajali as the last three personal practices (niyamas), is a set of synergistic tools that bring about inner change. It consists of tapas, svadhyaya, and isvara-pranidhana."[3]

Tapas (discipline), svadhyaya (self study), and ishvara pranidhana (trust, surrender) make up Kriya Yoga, and I offer them to you as a way to show up for this work.

TAPAS:
discipline, showing up,
consistent effort

Kriya Yoga

YOGA OF ACTION

SVADHYAYA:
self study, studying,
becoming the witness

ISHVARA
PRANIDHANA:
surrender, trust

We need tapas, discipline, in order to show up in the first place. When we set up consistent practices and habits, even on days when we are tired or not in the mood, we are leaning into the wisdom of tapas. Svadhyaya, self study, is both about learning from the yoga teachings, but in this context it's really about becoming a curious witness to our own experience. It's diving into the writing, the noticing, the reflection about how and why we are the way we are. The last, ishvara pranidhana, trust or surrender, is really about surrendering to the Divine, however you want to define that which is bigger than you. It can also be about surrendering and trusting the process. Trusting that you know enough to begin.[4]

In concert, these three show us a path. We commit to showing up with consistency, we get curious about our experience, and we trust that in doing so, we'll find more fulfillment and freedom.

In terms of the leadership themes, these are inspired by the 7 chakras, or energetic centers in the body. I am not going to make the scientific case for these or explain them in full detail - there are others who have done that. Again, please visit the sources. My hope is that you embody the mystery, try some practices, and know that we are planting seeds together.

Think of the leadership themes more as an organized way to explore different facets of who you are - in this particular season of your life. Each theme will bring in elements of nature, awaken aspects of our physical body, urge you to explore certain emotions or shadows of your past, and use all of that to support your evolution into your future. The fact that they are aligned to the chakras is a portal into the deeper wisdom of the yoga teachings, and of your own body.

Are you ready?

Leadership Intentions: "I Learn"

> "Let the power of intention lead the way."
>
> ~Sharon Salzberg

Where We Begin

Here we go....Leadership Intentions!

First of all, I'm so grateful you are here. This journey of growth - both for ourselves and the communities we serve - is best done in partnership. As you dive in, I hope you experience this book as a dialogue between you and I, and you and those you love. The fact that you said YES already communicates to your body, your mind and your heart that you are ready for the next level of this evolution and impact.

So let's get into it.

What's the big picture of where we're going? And where are we now?

I have organized this book like a yoga class. We begin with

intentions, we end with integrations. In between, we build from the ground up, from the most dense element to the lightest.

So, as we do with any good yoga practice, let's begin with our intentions.

We could think our way to an intention, but when we ground first in the body, we're able to access our unconscious minds, our intuition, our deeper levels of consciousness to arrive at this intention. I hope you allow yourself some time to engage in the yoga practice I've shared in this chapter, sit in meditation and let your intentions reveal themselves in their own time.

I'd love to share my intention with you as I offer this book:

INSPIRE, INFORM & EMPOWER

My *intention*, my prayer, for this experience together is....

- To catalyze changes that ripple far beyond these pages. I want the insights, the learnings, the healing that occurs in this book to change your life.

- I want it to change the way you show up for yourself and for those you impact in deeply beautiful ways.

- I want you to be able to say that you are not the same person you were when we started. That you have a deeper level of awareness, that you are crystal clear on your purpose, on how you access creativity, and that you are so confident in who you are.

- I hope that you have more self-compassion and therefore greater compassion for others as well. I want you to be able to speak your truth with love and clarity.

- I pray that you will know what tools and conditions allow you to access your intuition and that in doing so, you are able to turn your life experiences into wisdom with ease. I hope you remember that everything is connected and that insight shifts the way you see the world.

- In short, I want to empower you with the tools, strategies, knowledge and experiences to uplevel your life like never before. I hope to inspire you along the journey, to cheer you on, and create a safe, loving and joyful space for growth.

Setting Our Intention Matters

You know the phrase "where your attention goes, energy flows?"

To me, setting your intentions is directing your attention and your energy *on purpose*.

The best part is, it doesn't have to be complicated.

You can set your intention for any particular chunk of time - an hour in your day, a class you are leading or teaching, a workshop or professional development, in the morning before you dive into work, at the beginning of a new month or fresh season in your life.

Some examples I've heard or personally used:

- build strength

- kindness for myself and others

- show up with love

- presence

- embrace curiosity

- plan for the margins

- focus

- shift my perspective

- complete XYZ project with joy

- spaciousness

- stay with my breath

- receptivity

- gratitude

    and the list goes on and on and on...

You could set your intention for the month, for the year, you get the idea.

We live in a world that is constantly fighting for our attention.

It requires practice, and some discipline, to set our intentions and come back to them.

We can support ourselves in revisiting intentions with different types of "attention" tools.

- Visual reminders like sticky notes....*I'll write my intention somewhere I look every day.*

- Auditory tools like a timer....*I'll set a timer at noon each day to remind me to journal on my intention.*

- Connection to an existing routine...*when I brush my teeth, I will contemplate my intention.*

- Accountability tools (coach/friend/therapist, weekly reflection journal)...*I'll create a sacred time/place/person to ask me about what I'm learning about my intention*

- Physical space (sacred space)...*I'll create an area of my home that is JUST for this practice, when I see it and go there, what I do is XYZ...*

These are just some strategies to help you remember your intention. To remember where you want your energy to flow, and where you want your attention to go.

Depending on the parameters of the moment, setting intentions can vary in size, shape, scope and energy.

Here are a few ways you could think about setting your intentions as a leader:

- A word or phrase
- A longer mission statement
- A way of being
- A focus for a short time
- A life's work
- How you want to show up
- Who you want to be in a given context
- Something to remember
- Something to cultivate or embody
- Something to offer to the world/receive from the world

One of My Stories

Sometime in my late 20s, I began to shift from setting resolutions to creating intentions for the year - just **a word or a phrase.**

I distinctly remember a couple years in a row it was "create space".

I don't recall exactly what it meant. It might have been referring to something physical like "create space in my home" or something more emotional like "creating room in my heart". What I do know is the result.

The domino effect of setting this intention to "create space" was changing careers, ending a relationship, packing up my stuff and moving from Arizona to California with a vision but no plan.

I love this version of myself. The one that listens to her heart, doesn't need the details to be figured out, and deeply trusts. There are so many parts of myself that action like this scares - the part of me that loves to be a woman with a plan, the part that loves to ask all the questions and have the answers in hand.

The beauty of an intention is that it is not a concrete goal. It's an arrow that pulls our awareness in a direction, and remembers that anywhere we're trying to go requires us to place one foot in front of the other.

When I made this leap, the timing was anything but ideal. It was a peak recession era: 2010. Teachers were promised furlough days rather than raises. San Francisco prices were not what they are today, but they were certainly more than the cost of living in Arizona. I did not yet have a new job in San Francisco, but I had friends, the ocean, and the desire to be somewhere that felt more like me.

To me, that's what following our intuition feels like. That sense of conviction despite what some evidence might say.

Intuition and intentions are so connected! Often when we set intentions, it's this word or phrase - a whisper that emerges from the heart. Sometimes the intentions are small. *I want to cultivate strength in this practice. I want to embody kindness today.*

And sometimes they are our intentions for our whole lives. *I want to help people learn, heal and grow.*

It can feel daunting to call your life's intention out of thin air, and so we practice. We start small.

We start with a few minutes sitting in silence, asking ourselves simple questions.

It might sound like this:
- How does my body feel?
- How is the quality of my mind, my thoughts?
- What emotions are present in my heart?
- What do I need today?
- What do I want to offer to others? To the world today?

Then we listen.

Some days it might take a while to hear and feel a response. Others, it emerges loud and clear and immediate.

I promise you'll hear something. You'll hear that whisper, that word or phrase, and you can just start with that seed of an intention. We don't always need to know the endgame in order to get started. It is often enough to know *HOW* we want to begin.

Your Intentions & Reflections

Sitting here, as you are, I'll invite you to close your eyes in a moment and ask one of these simple questions.

- What is my intention in reading and working through this book?
- What is my intention as a leader (in my work, in my family, in the world?)
- How do I want to show up as I dive deeper into this journey?

My Reflections :

IT'S ALL CONNECTED

PROMPT:

My intention for this leadership and wellness journey is....

My Full Thoughts :

Now, shorten your extended thoughts into a phrase.

My Phrase :

Finally, condense everything into one word.

My Word :

Now, take some time to reflect on how your intention might look, feel and sound like on a day-to-day basis.

- What would it **feel** like to embody this intention?
- What would it **look** like to embody this intention?
- What would it **sound** like to embody this intention?
- What's one small way you could make your intention come alive for you (visual, audio, tactile)?

My Reflections :

Embodiment Practices

The meditation and yoga can be practiced separately, or in either order. Experiment and see what feels most supportive in initiating your intentions for this journey.

Meditation Script

Find a comfortable place to sit or lay in silence. Take a few deep breaths to calm and settle the body. Then invite a sense of peace to your mind as well.

This meditation practice will be simply time for you to contemplate your intention for this time together as you journey through this book.

As you breathe easily, repeat in your mind or outloud...what is my intention for this leadership journey?

Allow for silence, listen inward, and trust what arises. You are always allowed to let it evolve and change along the way.

When you have your intention, invite some movement back into the body, grab your journal and write down your thoughts.

Yoga Sequence

This particular yoga sequence is designed to offer a meditative quality to your intentions. By coming through nine sun salutations with full prostration, each time you lay everything down, you are symbolizing surrender. The palms are open, the forehead connects, and the entire front body - the part of ourselves we usually present to the world - is flat on the ground. The repetition is meant to use your intention like a mantra, focusing the mind, focusing your efforts, your attention, and your actions.

From the sun salutations, we move strategically up the energetic centers of the body. From the roots, the ground, the feet up to the crown of the head. It is enough to come into the poses and breathe. The shapes themselves are powerful, and when you focus on sensation, you give your body a chance to communicate what might need further investigation and love.

If you want to uplevel your experience, you can work with the affirmations that correspond to the different energetic centers - chakras - in the body. They will appear in a circle shape around the pose.

LEADERSHIP INTENTIONS
Yoga Sequence

CHILD'S POSE

CAT/COW FLOW

DOWNWARD DOG

IT'S ALL CONNECTED

SALUTATIONS BEGIN...

MOUNTAIN ANJALI MUDRA

MOUNTAIN UPWARD SALUTE

FORWARD FOLD

HALFWAY LIFT

PLANK

COBRA

FULL PROSTRATION

REPEAT SALUTATIONS
9X

DOWNWARD DOG

I belong.

I am grounded.

TREE

I flow.

I create.

GODDESS

WARRIOR TWO - R AND L

-or-

DOWNWARD DOG / VINYASA

DOWNWARD DOG

LOW LUNGE TWIST- R AND L

PLANK

I can.

I know who I am.

SIDE PLANK - R AND L

PLANK

DOWNWARD DOG

DOLPHIN

FOREARM PLANK

I love.

I offer / receive.

SPHINX

CHILD'S POSE

I speak.

I listen.

CAMEL

I see.

I trust.

HERO

IT'S ALL CONNECTED

SEATED TWIST

REVERSE PIGEON

I know.

I remember.

SAVASANA

plank

chaturanga

upward dog

downward dog

locust

cobra

cat / cow flow . . . . .

RESET . REPEAT .

Moving forward, a yoga sequence will appear in each chapter of the book. Throughout the book, each flow consists of four poses.

You'll see the phrase 'Reset . Repeat .' between each flow. Take a moment to reset your breath to movement before repeating the flow on the opposite side.

OPTIONS FOR RESET:

- chaturanga → upward dog → downward dog

- plank → cobra → downward dog

- plank → locust → downward dog

- cat / cow → downward dog

LEADERSHIP INTENTIONS

In Summary...

- Intentions are powerful ways to begin.

- Intentions can be for a single moment or a lifetime, and it might evolve as you do.

- An intention is a way of directing your energy and attention.

- Spend some time drafting your intention before diving into the next chapter.

PROMPTS FOR FURTHER REFLECTION

1. How are you engaging with your leadership intention this week? Describe a moment where you spent a little extra time with your intention this week and what the result was.

2. If your best friend were to describe you as a leader, what words would they use? How does it feel to see yourself as a leader through their eyes?

3. What is something this week that a past version of you would be SO excited about/proud of?

4. Consider how moving your body or sitting in stillness impacted your connection to your leadership this week.

My Reflections :

_____

_____

_____

_____

_____

_____

_____

_____

_____

_____

_____

_____

_____

_____

_____

_____

_____

_____

1 Lead with Purpose: "I Belong"

> "When you're clear on your values, you align your skills, time and energy to your purpose - and purposefulness is a key trait of the resilient."
>
> ~Elena Aguilar in *Onward*

Building Our Foundation

To talk about purpose is to talk about where we come from and where we are going. This inevitably leads us to family, home, what we value, what we had and what we lacked. The conditions for our understanding of love and belonging or our misperceptions about what we deserve in terms of safety, security and home. Given all that, it makes sense that the shadow side of this energy center is fear. Exploring the shadows will be an important part of learning in this theme, and will lay the groundwork for the themes that follow.

If that paragraph brought up some big emotions - I want to invite you to take some deep breaths, and be gentle with yourself as you proceed. The world at large is, and has been, in a root chakra crisis, and grounding our individual as well as collective energy is as complicated as it is important.

The element we will explore is earth, which is just so perfect. The ground beneath our feet. Our history. Our relationship to this entire planet. It's all here in the topic of Leading with Purpose. I hope this chapter grounds you. Makes you pause, take time outside, exhale more fully.

Knowing what our purpose is, let alone knowing how to lead from that purpose, is big. If it feels daunting, that's honestly a good sign that you are thinking in the right direction. We'll need both feet firmly planted on the earth as we explore how our past shapes our present and future. We'll explore how slowing down, getting curious about how we relate to our larger communities, and how being where we are all help us in getting clear on our purpose.

It's worth the time to dig deep, to understand the places where we've been in order to get clear about where we are going.

What Does it Mean to Lead with Purpose?

When we have clarity about who we are at a deep level - not necessarily who we are in response to early events that have occurred - we can feel anchored, ready to lead a life of purpose.

When we Lead with Purpose, we know why we are here. We are clear that we belong and that our soul has important work to do. We know our values, who we are in relation to our community. We know our role in the group.

In order to feel that sense of certainty, we must feel safe, secure, rooted to the here and now. As life continues to swirl and pull on our attention, we are focused on what matters to us, knowing that we have a finite amount of energy to use.

Leading with Purpose feels like one huge exhale that allows the body to relax into this exact moment, knowing that we are in the right place at the right time.

I imagine that if you are here, you know your purpose or have a deep desire to. Either way, you are perfectly on time.

One of my favorite ways to begin this work is to explore our values - in this particular season. It can help to list values professionally and personally, then notice where they do or do not overlap.

Mini exercise #1: Values

Read the following sentences, then close your eyes and FEEL the answer. Jot down whatever notes work for you.

- In my life, I value...
- Knowing that my time, energy and attention are precious resources, in an ideal world, I choose to spend them on....
- In this season of my life, what matters most to me is...
- I feel most like me when...
- What supports me in feeling my best is...

Use these prompts or you can also search a Values List, to create a list of your top values. Choose three to five, and then consider what they mean to you. Write about how this value shows up in your life.

Now, you might want to also make a list of where your time, energy and attention actually go, and notice any differences.

My Reflections : _____

_____

_____

_____

_____

_____

_____

_____

_____

_____

_____

_____

_____

_____

_____

_____

_____

_____

_____

_____

_____

_____

Knowing our top values increases our sense of fulfillment. When the way we spend our time is aligned with out values, we feel more at peace, more purposeful. When they are misaligned, we are likely to feel stagnant, unhappy or dissatisfied with life.

Similarly, when we are clear on our purpose, we can live a life of deep meaning. That's why we're starting here, at the root, with knowing our purpose.

Mini exercise #2: Purpose

Again, tap into your breath, and without overthinking it, respond to the following prompts. Let yourself be surprised by what comes through.

- In this life, I'm here to....
- My purpose in this life is to...
- If I could share just one message with the world, it would be...
- All those who love me most, would say my purpose in this life is to...
- My soul feels most aligned when...

My Reflections :
_____
_____
_____
_____
_____

Notice what the answers were. Anything you didn't expect?

It's so easy for our conscious minds to get caught up in the labels of a certain job, role or title. But our purpose is deeper than that. It's our life's work. It will adjust, change, shift in how it shows up and presents itself, but the core of it will remain.

I've always done some aspect of supporting others to heal, grow and learn. Whether that was babysitting, caring for my younger siblings, being the designated driver in a group of sorority sisters, teaching middle school, coaching teachers, teaching yoga classes, etc. - I see evidence of this nurturing quality everywhere. Did I also work in dozens of restaurants and other odd jobs? Sure. Did those light up my soul and offer that feeling of "I'm in the right place at the right time"? They did not.

Our bodies give us so many clues as to whether or not we are on the right path. So as we dive into the ways to work with the theme of Leading with Purpose, I invite you to make a habit of checking in with your body's signals.

In order to do this chapter - this topic - justice, it might take longer than others. Like the base of the pyramid, I want to set our foundation strong. If there are exercises or prompts or stories that bring up a lot for you, or seem to ask you to slow down to make meaning, please listen to that.

I'd like to tell you a few stories, one about my childhood, and one about early motherhood, because the two tales are connected.

Before we do that, I want to give you the high level information about the energetic center that corresponds with this leadership theme. The root chakra.

On the next page, you'll find a "chakra chart". It includes smaller details about the energetic center, such as what part of the body corresponds to that chakra, as well as larger themes that relate to how we can heal and lead. Get curious about what piques your interest and what resonates. As you continue reading, I hope you notice how those themes reappear in the stories that follow.

Name	Root chakra (muladhara chakra)
Location in the body	Base of the spine, perineum
Parts of the body related to this chakra	Legs, feet, rectum, spinal column, lower intestinal tract, bones, teeth, immune system
Color	Red
Stone to work with	Red jasper, hematite
Element	Earth
When this chakra is *balanced*, you feel...	• Grounded and safe in the body • Stable and secure • Strong foundation • Calm nervous system and demeanor • Rooted in the here and now
When this chakra is *out of balance*, you feel...	• Ungrounded and not in the body • Anxious and worried • Fearful about having basic needs met • Insecure and unsure • Lacking - in mindset and behaviors

This chakra helps you *heal* **by...**	• Exploring your familial roots and the impact they have on your life now. • Calming your nervous system so you have a steady and safe foundation in all spaces you enter. • Healing from any primary loss or familial fractures. • Revising mindsets around financial scarcity.
This chakra helps you *lead* **by...**	• Understanding your home, your family, your community, and your place in society. • Recognizing where you come from impacts how you show up. • Connecting to and meeting your basic needs. • Moving in a way that allows for presence.
Shadow to explore	Fear
Affirmations	• I belong. • I am here. • I am safe. • I am grounded. • I am here on purpose. • I am home in my body. • I am rooted. • I am steady.
Ways of being	Grounded, patient, calm, present, purposeful

Whew! Take a deep breath, feel your feet. That is a lot of information. Notice what it brought up in your body as you read through that list. Did you receive any insights from your body? Any images or flashes pop up from your childhood or about your current basic needs? Ground yourself in the idea that when our needs are met, we thrive and live out our purpose. When they are not met or we're not able to get them met, we experience suffering.

I invite you to take a minute and jot some notes down before jumping back in.

My Reflections :

Earth Element

The element associated with Leading with Purpose, and the root chakra, is EARTH. It is steady, rooted, and grounded. Take a moment and imagine your feet on the earth - solid, strong, steady. Maybe it's grassy fields, maybe it's a dirt path. Either way, imagine you could lay your whole body down and feel the support of this earth. Did you exhale? I did as I was writing this.

When we tap into the earth element, we remember that we are held. We let ourselves relax into the support of gravity, the solid structure underneath us. That allows us to remember the solid structures within ourselves. The bones, the feet, the legs. They all help us move about in our days, show us where we are in time and space, where we belong in this moment.

The steady and slow element of earth is an invitation to slow down and take your time. The pace of nature around us teaches us about the change of seasons, the importance of waiting in winter in order to fully appreciate the bounty of spring. Feeling into the seasons of change within ourselves reminds us we don't need to be in such a rush all the time. We too can move a little slower.

Consider children for a moment - they LOVE to take shoes off, and run around outside, dirt smudged all over them. When was the last time you did that?

One beautiful quality about embodying the earth element is that the ways it can show up are so different. The red rocks in Arizona are so different from the sandy beaches in Florida are so different from the granite giants in Yosemite. The earth element in you will shift too. There might be seasons where your solid foundation has a more shifting quality to it, like the sand. Others where it's sparkling like diamonds or tough like granite.

Being around and connecting to the earth beneath you, as well as the trees around you, have numerous health benefits. Research supports what we already know, spending time in nature, specifically forest bathing or in "green spaces", reduces feelings of stress and anxiety. [5]

Part of why this element is so foundational is because it connects us to a feeling of safety, and "being able to feel safe with other people is probably the single most important aspect of mental health; safe connections are fundamental to meaningful and satisfying lives."[6]

There are so many ways to connect to this solid quality. Maybe you are called to embody the earth element by remembering how good it feels to slow down. To appreciate the structures within and around you. To notice how setting a foundation for your day, your relationships or even creating a project plan can help everything that follows. As you explore the grounding nature of earth, take your time and truly plant the deep roots for your growth.

Earth

solid
steady
grounded
slow
strong
stable
reminds us to set roots and take our time

Pause & Process

At this point, you've taken in a lot of information! I'm going to invite you to pause and process for a moment. Use the space below to note five takeaways or write some questions that may be swirling around for you related to the theme of purpose.

An idea resonating with me is...

1

A question I have is...

2

I'm learning...

3

I'm wondering about...

4

A line of text that is sticking with me is...

5

Your Healing & Leadership: Application of "Leading with Purpose"

Understanding Our Foundation Matters

You may have heard the analogy of inviting your inner child into the back seat of the car, to let her know she's seen and loved, but you are not handing her the keys to the car. You, the steady, sturdy adult, are at the wheel.

When we practice deep presence, we realize that past versions of ourselves are always with us, informing what lights us up, what triggers our nervous system, what feels like home.

To do the work of Leading with Purpose, we have to invite in these past versions of ourselves - not to run the show, but to acknowledge their existence and impact on how we show up.

I want to acknowledge and create some space at the table for three year old Jess. The version of me that lost her father, first in small moments as my mother made the tough decision to move to a new city so she could provide financially for our family of four, and then all together when his life ended at just 32.

As I write this, my own daughter is already older than I was, and my heart literally cannot fathom what this experience was like for my mother, for three- year- old me, and my two- year- old sister. The confusion, the instability, the grief, the devastation. My heart breaks with compassion for each of us, and for my young father - who might have felt like he had no other options. At 32, life is still just beginning.

To lose a parent - at any age, in any way - is life altering. To experience divorce, housing or financial instability, absent parents or turbulence in caregiver relationships - it all impacts our ability to feel safe where we are. To know where we belong, where we come from, and what we deserve.

I can only speak to my own lived experience, and hope that in doing so, I create pockets for you to explore the impact of your roots as well.

It's impossible for me to tell that story of these primary years from the perspective of me when I was little, because I don't remember. Even so, that early loss left a mark, a gaping hole, exposed roots, that impacted me in ways I'm still unpacking and healing today.

Throughout different stages of my life, I have felt the reverberations of this rocky foundation. I have spent so much time asking questions, searching for stability, desiring answers to some deeply rooted inquiries such as: Am I worthy of love? Do I belong? Am I enough, just as I am?

It's vulnerable to write these down on paper - to offer them to you.

But my guess is that at one point or another, you too have wondered a version of those questions.

They tend to come up when we begin something. A new school. A new relationship. A new job or role in our family. A new version of our reality.

They also tend to come up when we end something. A chapter of our life. A relationship or friendship. A career.

These questions about who I am and where do I belong in this context are ways we connect ourselves to our purpose. Like roots of a tree, the answers spread deep and wide and secure us in a spot in a way that says "I've got you". You belong right here.

To lose a parent, or to experience lack in your basic needs like food, shelter, or love shakes these roots. It's hard to know you are safe when your survival feels threatened.

As I've navigated relationships - friendships and romantic ones - I've learned to be present with this primary loss. To invite it to the table and listen to what it has to say. To notice when my nervous system feels threatened or when it feels safe. I've taken time to relearn, recreate and redefine safety and security. They are calming. They are comforting.

I've practiced acknowledging the loss, the hurt, the pain, the impact that it has on how I mother, and how I lead, rather than pushing it aside. Allowing more space for healing instead of ignoring.

I've chosen to slow down, to be as present with my daughter as I can, to choose grounding movements, practices, let emotions come through, and connect to the ancient wisdom of nature.

I'll dive into these practices in more detail, but the image that I hope stays with you is the roots - the trees. The steady energy of laying and nurturing a foundation before the leaves and flowers can bloom.

Applications to Your Healing

THE ROOT CHAKRA HELPS YOU HEAL BY...

- Exploring your familial roots and the impact they have on your life now. Therapy, intentional reflection, journaling, healing conversations are just some of the ways you can begin to rewrite the stories from when you were young.

- Calming your nervous system, often by slowing down and breathing deeply, so you have a steady and safe foundation in all spaces you enter.

- Reparenting, or tending to the needs of your inner child, can be a way to prioritize your wellbeing and heal from any primary loss or familial fractures.

- Revising mindsets around financial scarcity to see the world and its resources as abundant.

Take some time to jot down any thoughts, reactions, sensations or emotions that are present in your experience **related to your healing**. Notice anything that is coming up now that you might want to revisit later before we dive into exploring the shadow of this energetic center.

My Reflections :

Exploring the Shadow: Fear

When I first became a new mom, a feeling I didn't anticipate was fear.

I was so ready to be a mom. I thought my years of being an educator had more than prepared me to intuitively know what my daughter needed, and be able to joyfully provide that for her.

What I didn't anticipate was experiencing two pregnancy losses in the year prior to getting pregnant with my now school-aged daughter. Those losses rocked my foundation. Pulled my roots up if you will. I was mistrustful of my own body. I was afraid it would betray me, and despite countless hours of intentional work throughout my pregnancy, I don't think I fully exhaled until she arrived safely in my arms.

The tricky thing about fear - and trust - is that they both are a type of faith. We're putting our energy, our attention, and our belief that something will or will not happen into the unknown future. I'm either afraid things won't work out, or I can trust that they will.

In those first few months, I didn't want to be away from her. It was a combination of this fear of losing her and my own losses that I experienced as a child. The primary loss of my father was all of a sudden front and center for me - the family foundation being unstable and needing to reestablish the roots.

As I learned more about how this wound shows up, I realized this fear wasn't a present day fear - it was a younger version of me showing up and asking for attention. My three year old self wanted to know that she was safe, loved, and that she belonged. This understanding grew my compassion. For myself, for my family, for anyone who has lost someone at any age and is trying to make sense of what life looks like afterwards.

I practiced slowing down. Giving myself - present and young Jess - time and space to feel her feelings. To acknowledge them and give *them room. To say, wow - it was so hard to experience that loss. You must have been so confused. So heartbroken. No wonder you feel a little worried now. It's okay to take the time you need, to focus on your breath, to speak it out loud, to write it down, and then invite some of it to be let go.*

It takes space to process and let go. Room we don't always have in an obvious way. The conditions of the pandemic gave me unanticipated, and unprecedented space, and I chose to use it to heal. Even now, with a busy schedule and an active preschooler, I start here. With grounding. With belonging. With purpose.

Knowing where we come from, and the wounds that may be present is an essential part of knowing how to show up intentionally for our loved ones. When I take the time to honor the needs of previous versions of myself, to attend to the fear and the worries - I create more space to show up with love for myself, my family, and my work in the world.

It's okay to take the time to cry it out in the shower, feel more cleansed, and go hug my daughter, take a walk in the redwoods, and breathe deeply.

When I do that - prioritize grounding, slowing down and planting my roots - I am able to transform fear into trust. I am able to place that faith into a more hopeful future, and more accurately see my present. I clear the lens of my own life, and am able to see myself as a mama who is safe, laying a foundation of love for her family, and healing as she goes.

Let me clear - this exploration isn't an exercise in blame or shame. Life happens as it happens. Unfortunately, tragic things happen to people everyday. And so do beautiful things. I deeply believe everyone is doing the best they can with the tools they have at the time, and at their disposal.

I had the privilege of time and space to heal because of the hard work done by my mother so many years ago. You may have more or less work to do around your roots because of your parents and their experiences, and their parents and their experiences.

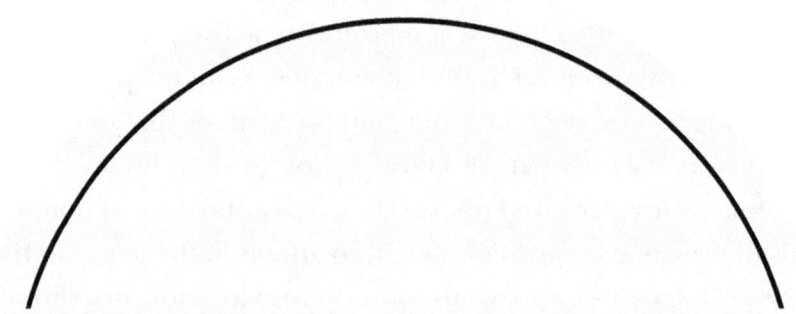

"When I prioritize grounding, slowing down and planting my roots--I am able to transform fear into trust."

Exploring this chakra is an opportunity to get curious around your relationship to **safety, belonging, and purpose.** Is it easy for you to find yourself in a new place and assume good things will unfold? Or does it require a lot of intentional work for your nervous system to ground first?

My Reflections :

Your healing and relationship to the root chakra paints the backdrop of how you show up as a leader.

Applications to Your Leadership

THE ROOT CHAKRA HELPS YOU LEAD BY...
• Creating a clear and rooted mission for yourself and your work is the foundation for ALL that you do.   • Knowing your values and how they guide your purpose in the world gives you a life full of meaning.   • Tuning into your self care - prioritizing your wellness so you can show up each day and thrive in your work.   • Starting meetings or workshops with grounding breaths with clear intentions and agendas helps participants feel safe, secure, and able to be present.

On the following page, take some time to jot down any thoughts, reactions, sensations or emotions that are present in your experience **related to your leadership**. Note any ideas, connections or musings you want to remember before we think about specific moments where you and I both have chosen to Lead with Purpose.

My Reflections :

A Moment I Decided to Lead with Purpose

There are likely countless moments where you have Led with Purpose. To me, this looks like orienting ourselves to know where we belong in our community. To intentionally pause and ask "Who am I and what makes my unique perspective of value in the larger community?"

When I was in a moment of decision, mid-pandemic, with a 2 year old, trying to decide how to re-engage with the "traditional" workforce, I had the opportunity to step back and look at my experience, gifts, values, skills, passions....to consider what work felt meaningful to me. What work would feel like an authentic expression of my value to offer into the world?

Was I an effective instructional coach? Yes, absolutely.

Can I make a beautiful spreadsheet? You bet.

I naturally gravitated towards what was familiar - what I had just done. It's easy to do this. There is immediate proof that success would be likely.

In the time and space that lockdown provided, I was able to dive even deeper. I considered what moments stood out to me where I felt like my soul was in the right place at the right time.

- When I was coaching people in a way that invited their whole selves to the table.
- Where I talked with teachers about their goals for math instruction *and* how they were settling into the new team dynamics.
- When I coached a veteran teacher to reignite their love of learning *and* held space for them to share about the joys/struggles of being a parent while working an intense job.
- When I developed leaders with concrete leadership skills *and* intentionally led conversations about imposter syndrome, the emotions required to lead your peers and how to identify their strengths while they did that.

- When I knew that a teacher needed to take our coaching session outside, or encouraged them to eat lunch, or set boundaries around work at home.

I recognized how holistic my approach to coaching was. And how what I really craved was to be able to support these developing leaders in their wellness in addition to their leadership skills.

This is how "Lead and Be Well", my coaching business, was born.

I knew that my purpose was at this intersection of leadership coaching and wellness, because of my own lived experience. In order to be the leader that I am meant to be, I have to take care of myself, and I love encouraging others to do the same.

Feeling into the steady YES that thrums inside me when I do this work, and feeling the calm my nervous system experiences...that's the data I first look to in order to know if I'm on the right track. To know that I am in the right place, doing the right work, at the right time.

One of Your Stories

- What do you want to say about your roots and how it impacts your purpose as a leader in your life now?

- Write a story about belonging. What values are present? Who is there? What contributes to experiencing a sense of belonging in your community?

- Think of a time either when you felt really balanced in this first chakra or this aspect of yourself or a time when you felt safe, rooted, grounded, clear on your sense of belonging (in yourself, your community, and/or in your environment).

- Think of a moment that brought healing to a younger version of you. It might be a moment where you recognized a past hurt, something missing, or you identified a puzzle piece that needed to be attended to related to your sense of belonging. It might be about your sense of safety, your ability to be grounded, present and purposeful.

_____

_____

_____

_____

_____

_____

_____

Embodiment Practices

The meditation and yoga can be practiced separately, or in either order. Experiment and see what feels most supportive in grounding you in the here and now.

Meditation Script
(tap into grounding and purpose)

Find a comfortable place to sit or even lay down. Take a few moments to connect to whatever parts of your body are touching the earth. Create more connection here. Either through surface area, through giving gravity permission to gently pull the bones closer to the ground, or through your exhales. Take a few deep breaths, letting your exhales be twice as long as the inhales. Allow each exhale to be an invitation to get closer to the ground, to put something down, to soften.

Imagine that your body could connect deeper beneath the ground. As if roots were sprouting from your body and moving underneath the floorboards, the foundation of your home, into the dirt, the rocks, the layers of the earth. Feel into that sensation. Tap into the cooling, steady, ancient wisdom of the deepest roots you can visualize.

Let the breath slow down even more. Long, slow, deep exhales.

Now imagine that those roots that are sprouting from you are reminding you of your family. Your ancestors. Your first understanding of home and safety. Track your body for sensation. Imagine that your roots represented your values and your deep beliefs about what matters most in this world. Imagine they were a clear path about how you want to show up, and where you belong.

Whose roots mingle with yours? What do these roots intuitively tell you about why you are here, what you are meant to do, and where you belong? (pause and give time to notice what arises)

Begin to bring your awareness back into your body, here on the earth. Deepen your breath and bring some small movements into your fingers and toes, ankles and wrists. Blink the eyes and come back into space. Notice how you feel.

Journal about any images, emotions, thoughts, or ideas that came forth.

My Reflections :

How to Practice

Throughout this simple flow, move slowly to help embody the earth element. Feel your feet and your legs. Notice how the bones stack, and how gravity impacts the body.

Leading with Purpose is all about setting your foundation, so consider how you are creating a steady base through whatever is in contact with the ground in each posture. Allow this particular sequence to be grounding.

Warm up - Sun Salutation A

1 MOUNTAIN

2 FORWARD FOLD

3 HALFWAY LIFT

4 PLANK

REPEAT 5X

5 DOWNWARD FACING DOG

6 HALFWAY LIFT

7 FORWARD FOLD

8 MOUNTAIN ANJALI MUDRA

Flows

1A RUNNER'S LUNGE

1B LOW LUNGE

1C SIMPLE TWIST

1D PLANK

RESET. REPEAT.

2A LIZARD

2B LIZARD + TWIST

2C LIZARD + QUAD STRETCH

2D PLANK

RESET. REPEAT.

3A WARRIOR TWO

3B TRIANGLE

3C WIDE LEGGED FOLD

3D MOUNTAIN

RESET. REPEAT.

4A HIGH LUNGE

4B WARRIOR THREE

4C HIGH LUNGE

4D PYRAMID

RESET. REPEAT.

Cool Down

1 TREE

2 MALASANA

3 HAPPY BABY

4 REST

how to engage with the theme of

PURPOSE

body

- Move slowly and with purpose.
- Feel your feet and legs, bones and teeth.
- Notice your surroundings with all of your senses.
- Honor your body's basic needs like sleep and nourishing meals.
- Breathe slow and deep.

mind

- Learn about where you come from and your family history.
- Explore quiet moments.
- Inquire about how your community impacts how you see the world.
- Reflect on where you feel a sense of purpose and belonging.
- Repeat and meditate on your affirmation.

soul

- Write a letter to your younger self, and have them write one to you.
- Post a younger picture of you somewhere you can see it often.
- Journal about your values and living in alignment with them.
- Create a grounding ritual practice to start and/or end your day.
- Spend time in nature.

work

- Consider your deepest purpose in your work, family and life.
- Slow things down.
- Align your priorities and daily actions with your larger mission.
- Include breathwork before or between meetings/projects.
- Build a safe and welcoming community at work.

Leading
with
PURPOSE
means...

- Embodying the quality of the earth element to remember to tend to your roots first.
- Identifying what you value and why you value it.
- Knowing where you came from, where you are now, and where you want to go.
- Having a steady, sturdy foundation for safety, security and belonging.
- Knowing where you belong.
- Knowing who you are in relation to your community, and the larger context.

PROMPTS FOR FURTHER REFLECTION

1. Choose something to slow down this week that you normally do fast. Experiment with moving and thinking slowly - write down any reflections.

2. Look through your week with the lens of purpose - what shifts for you when you think about *why* you are doing what you are doing?

3. Choose one of your values this week and notice how often you align your activities, time, energy and attention with that value. What do you notice?

4. Consider how moving your body or sitting in stillness has impacted your connection to your leadership this week.

My Reflections : _____

_____

_____

_____

_____

_____

_____

_____

_____

_____

_____

_____

_____

_____

_____

_____

_____

_____

_____

IT'S ALL CONNECTED

P U R P O S E

In Summary...

- Leading with Purpose correlates to the root chakra.

- Exploring, embodying and spending time close to the earth element can deepen your connection to this theme.

- Learning about, healing and loving your foundation, your history and inviting it into your present day life is a way to support your growth in this energy center.

- Exploring your purpose, your fears, and your roots is huge. Take your time here.

2 Lead with Creativity: "I Flow"

> "You can do it like it's a great weight on you, or you can do it like it's a dance."
>
> ~Ram Dass

Feeling Our Flow

If Leading with Purpose is setting our foundation, creating the structure in which you want to live our lives, then Leading with Creativity is the abundant river that flows throughout that structure.

These two energetic centers of the body can be explained as the bowl filled with water, or the banks to the river, or the rocky coast meeting the waves of the ocean.

Leading with Purpose and Leading with Creativity go together like the perfect pairing, in sweet oppositional balance.

We need to have our foundation rooted enough that our body and our nervous system feel settled so that our energy can flow.

Creativity, pleasure and emotions then have permission to flow like the tides. With that permission, we can recognize, celebrate and find joy in creating within this sacred container of our purpose - guilt free. We can give birth to ideas, new ways of being, and sometimes humans.

Leading with Creativity is all about bringing forth and allowing energy to flow with ease.

The energetic center we'll explore is related to our one-on-one relationships, boundaries, emotions, creativity, pleasure, and our ability to feel. Creativity is deeply connected to emotions and intuition. As we dive in, we will explore our emotions, how we can ride the waves, but not get swept away, how we can use emotions to inspire our creations.

We'll explore the shadow - guilt - that can emerge when we set boundaries, ask for what we want, and create from our deepest desires.

The element is water, and I hope that you let these words wash over you in this chapter. That you sink into a state of flow, imagine yourself (or actually go) by your favorite body of water as you read. I hope the steady rhythm of the waves - real or imagined - support your ability to tap into your own creative flow.

What Does it Mean to Lead with Creativity?

Leading with Creativity is all about accessing a state of flow - in our work, in our relationships, in our innovative endeavors. It's about how we adapt to the moment and understand the cyclical nature of our bodies and the world.

It's about feeling, naming, processing, understanding and letting go of emotions. It's about tapping into intuition and feeling rather than needing logic to always be the driver in decision making processes.

When we Lead with Creativity, we get clear with the boundaries we have (or need) in place to support our energy. We notice when our energy spills out in all directions, or gets stuck and inhibits our ability to enjoy life or create. If and when we experience guilt, the shadow of the sacral chakra, we recognize the societal conditioning or life experiences that are causing the guilt, and find ways to reconnect with our innate right to experience pleasure.

Mini exercise #1:
Connect to Emotions

Name as many emotions as you can. Write them down.

My Reflections :

Notice what your relationship is with these emotions. Track your body for any sensation that comes up as a result of even naming those emotions. Look again at your list, and reflect on how you feel as you connect with each emotion. (i.e. do you view any as "good" or "bad"?)

My Reflections : _____

_____

_____

_____

This is where the shadow, guilt, can often creep in. Guilt for feeling a certain way, when we are "supposed" to feel another. For example, if we are taught that we should always feel busy, a little stressed and *definitely* productive, feeling relaxed and joyful might trigger a sense of guilt.

What if, instead, we understand emotions as transient, human experiences that will move through everyone at one point or another. That they are separate from and do not define us. That they can be processed and moved through. That they can be observed, witnessed, and deserve acknowledgement for the information they are trying to convey.

What would be possible if we viewed emotions as data, rather than attaching our identity to them?

Brene Brown wrote an entire book about emotions because understanding what they are and how to work with them is so essential to being human. In her introduction to *Atlas of the Heart* she writes, "to form meaningful relationships with others, we must first connect with ourselves, but to do either, we must first establish a common understanding of the language of emotion and human experience."[7] If you haven't read it yet, I highly recommend it.

Leading with Creativity is the permission slip to tap into what you really want to bring into the world!

What do you want to create? What are you here to bring into the world?

If you left guilt at the door, and truly connected with your creative energy that is aligned with your purpose, what would abundance and success look and feel like in your life?

Mini exercise #2: Imagine Success and Abundance

In the space that follows, imagine what success and abundance, aligned with your purpose, looks like, sounds like and feels like in this season of your life and/or leadership.

- What is it you want to create, bring forth, or express in this life?
- List out categories for yourself, draw a picture, make a collage, and/or write words.
- Imagine expansively here, as if you could create life totally on your terms.
- Without allowing any "shoulds" to creep in, create the most beautiful version of what you want. Dream big, let it flow, take your time.

Notice how you feel. Hold on to this dream. By writing it down, you are already opening up the pathway for it to come true.

Then, when you're ready, let's learn more about this energetic center of the body - the sacral chakra.

My Reflections :

Name	**Sacral chakra (svadhisthana chakra)**
Location in the body	Below the naval, low belly, sacrum
Parts of the body related to this chakra	Sexual organs, hips, pelvic area, intestines and bladder, kidneys
Color	Orange
Stone to work with	Citrine, carnelian
Element	Water
When this chakra is *balanced*, you feel...	• Energized, refreshed and creative • Able to access a flow state • Deserving of and able to receive joy, pleasure, abundance • Satisfied in your emotional needs • Supported by boundaries
When this chakra is *out of balance*, you feel...	• Tired, fatigued or stuck • Lacking in desire and pleasure • Depleted by lack of boundaries • Uninspired • Dysregulated emotionally, or numb

This chakra helps you *heal* **by...**	• Naming, feeling and moving through your emotions. • Recognizing what conditions allow you to go with the flow of life. • Understanding what allows or inhibits your creativity. • Exploring present and past one-on-one relationship dynamics and the impact they have on you now.
This chakra helps you *lead* **by...**	• Honoring your one-on-one relationships through supportive boundaries. • Connecting to your creativity and intuition. • Finding energetic flow in your work and life. • Accepting change and transformation as a natural part of life.
Shadow to explore	Guilt
Affirmations	• I create. • I am creative. • I flow. • I feel. • I honor others but not before myself. • I deserve joy. • I have boundaries that support me. • I am abundant.
Ways of being	Creative, curious, joyful, flexible. expressive

Even the mention of the word boundary can bring up a lot for some people. Let alone guilt.

Notice what it brought up in your body as you read through that list. Did you receive any insights from your body? Any images, emotions or flashes pop up from your life or about what you deserve? Reflect on the idea that when we stay in the flow of life, we thrive and can create. When our energy and emotions are not honored, we can feel depleted.

Here's an invitation to take a minute and jot some notes down before jumping back in.

My Reflections :

Water Element

The element associated with Leading with Creativity, and the sacral chakra, is WATER. It is fluid, creative, and abundant.

As beings that are mostly water, living on a floating rock, whose surface is 71% covered by water, this is an important element to feel into.[8]

We need to drink a certain amount of water each day and nourish ourselves with hydrating foods in order to feel our best. We use water to bathe, clean aspects of our homes, water our plants, clean our cars, the list goes on. We can notice water as it falls from the sky, melts from the glaciers, gathers as dew, forms as fog, courses as rivers, reflects as lakes or crashes along the shore. It's all around us, and presents differently for each of us, depending where we are and the season we are in.

Take a moment to imagine all the ways that water shows up in your life - daily or throughout the course of a month. Where do you interact with water without even thinking about it, and where do you intentionally seek it out? How do you feel when you immerse yourself in it or listen to the sounds it creates? What does it remind you of?

When we connect with the water element, we remember to flow.

We notice how life is constantly changing and shape shifting. The fluid nature gives us permission to evolve. We remember how good it feels when we are hydrated, our bodies and brains function more optimally, and we can move with more ease, internally and about our day. We give ourselves permission to feel that good! We deserve to - it's in our very nature.

The water element is connected to the ability to feel our emotions, access our intuition and go with the flow. With the structure provided by the earth element - the natural boundaries, we can then soften into this feminine energy and allow emotions to rise and fall. The transient nature of water invites presence, so we can tap into our sense of feeling and intuiting our way through the world.

I'm sure you have felt the calm that radiates in your being around water, and research supports it. Often called "blue spaces", studies show that "being near water stimulates our senses, which can be psychologically healing."[9]

The different ways water can show up in your life are seemingly endless.

Maybe you are called to embody the power of the ocean in the way it can crash along the rocky shores of the Pacific Coast, or maybe it's more gentle lapping waves of a lake. Maybe it's the curious, creative flow of a river as it weaves its way through rocks and trees. Maybe it's the nourishing in and outside of your own body, the intimate way you hydrate and clean your own being. Maybe it's just permission to change your mind or protect your energy with stronger boundaries so it doesn't spill out all over the floor. Maybe it's playing with what it feels like to spend a day moving, moment to moment, asking the question, "what do I feel like next?"

Water

fluid
flexible
emotional
transient
flowing
ever-changing
reminds us to go with the flow

Pause & Process

At this point, you've taken in a lot of information! I'm going to invite you to pause and process for a moment. Use the space below to note five takeaways or write some questions that may be swirling around for you related to the theme of creativity.

An idea resonating with me is...

1

A question I have is...

2

I'm learning...

3

I'm wondering about...

4

A line of text that is sticking with me is...

5

Your Healing & Leadership:
Application of "Leading with Creativity"

Feeling Our Flow Matters

There's this hike I love just north of the Golden Gate Bridge. It's not too strenuous, there are a few different paths you can take depending on the vistas you want or the mood you are in.

Regardless of the path you take, at a certain point the trail curves and the ocean is revealed. I always pause and take a deep breath. The sight of the vast expanse of water invites me into a more relaxed state almost immediately.

I could sit or walk or practice yoga on this beach for hours, watching the waves flow in. They chase each other a bit, but respectfully. Each wave has its turn, its moment to shine, then it ebbs back and lets the next one go.

The slight incline of the beach and the rocky cliffs on either side create this natural boundary. The water can flow without wiping it all out. It's both wild and contained. Unique and predictable.

I can't help but dream on this hike.

Creativity and intuition swirl inside of me. My heart and mind wander between the biggest hopes I have in life and the details of a particular project or the answer to a question I've been stuck on. The freedom of being by the ocean seems to unlock a state of flow in my consciousness.

Who I am seems to flow more easily as well.

"Look at the waves," my soul seems to say, "it's not so hard to understand. We ebb, we flow. We create, we dance, we feel, we change. Everything changes, so why do you try to hold on so tightly? Why not, instead, create some natural boundaries, and then let things flow?"

The ocean reminds me to flow with ease and feel my feelings without guilt.

Allowing myself time to feel my feelings can often feel like an indulgence - have you ever felt that way? As if there isn't time for that, or what's the point?

In my first years of motherhood, I learned so much about the benefits of feeling our feelings, allowing them to be acknowledged, and letting them go - this is truly the only way to release them and not perpetually spin the same loops over and over. When we soften around any gripping on the emotion, and let it out rather than try to hold it in, it can actually move on. Return to the ocean.

I, unfortunately, don't live at this beach. And neither do you.

I live in a house, in a city, with a job and a life, in a society that loves productivity and urgency. And you likely have some similar situation.

But we can tap into this fluidity - we can create space for energy to flow through our homes, and within our bodies.

We can create natural boundaries for our time, our relationships, our energy, our work, our calendars and then let creativity flow within those spaces. We can create the conditions to feel our feelings, to explore movement and art and remember that everything changes.

Applications to Your Healing

THE SACRAL CHAKRA HELPS YOU HEAL BY...

- Naming, feeling and moving through your emotions. Deepening your intelligence and fluency with emotions, as well as ways to release them, are potent ways to heal.

- Recognizing what conditions, within yourself and around you, allow you to go with the flow of life.

- Understanding what allows or inhibits your creativity, pleasure and ability to receive abundance.

- Exploring present and past one-on-one relationship dynamics and the impact they have on you now, specifically learning to identify the relationships that nourish you, the ones that drain you, and the ones that would benefit from boundaries.

Take some time to jot down any thoughts, reactions, sensations or emotions that are present in your experience **related to your healing**. Notice anything that is coming up now that you might want to revisit later before we dive into exploring the shadow of this energetic center.

My Reflections :

Exploring the Shadow: Guilt

As women, we're told from a very young age that being able to produce children is just part of the deal. Whether we are told that in explicit words or just by what is modeled and shown all around us...motherhood is the "norm" and arguably the "ideal" that we are sold.

Women deal with guilt related to reproduction in countless ways.

We live in a time where a woman's right to choose is literally up for debate. Women who decide to live child-free often feel pressure to defend this choice.

And then on the other hand, for women who are struggling to conceive or sustain pregnancies, the routes they often need to take are incredibly expensive, emotionally taxing, and so vulnerable.

Then add in the complexities related to *how* we decide to work and parent. There are endless combinations, and you can find a cheerleader and critic for each one.

It's no wonder this energetic center of the body needs so much love.

The second baby I lost was just 10 weeks in utero, and I found out on New Year's Eve 2018. I had just returned home from Arizona where I spent the week sharing the ultrasound picture - *the good news!* - with friends and family. I was so relieved that my body was in fact, not broken. That the first time had been some weird fluke, but *no worries, all was now well.*

Hearing the silence as the OB/GYN listened for a heartbeat was the longest moment of my life. I didn't want to believe this was really happening. Again.

How didn't I know?

How disconnected was I from what was happening in my own body?

Not only was I wracked with grief, but there was a pervasive guilt as well.

Was it my fault?

Did I wait too long to start?

Did I twist too much, or eat the wrong thing? Did I rest too much or not enough? Was I too stressed? Did I not sleep enough or maybe I slept in the wrong position?

I felt numb.

I bought myself flowers, my favorite cupcakes and shared the news with two friends who were planning to come over to celebrate a relaxing New Year's Eve.

Yes - I still wanted them to come. I needed them to.

And then I cried.

I gave myself time to cry with my husband, my mom, and several of my best friends who lived far away.

It had taken a lot of courage and hope to try again - and I had hoped. That had felt dangerous to do, but I'd done it, and I was crushed.

I knew this time that I needed to seriously attend to my healing - body, mind and heart. And so I took time over the next few days, weeks and months.

The guilt that kept me from advocating for the time to heal the first go around felt different this time. I knew that I needed and deserved time to heal, so I let my boss know that I needed the week following winter break off, and then I settled into the process of healing, knowing I had two full weeks ahead of me. At once, an incredibly more spacious amount of time compared to the three days the first time, and also not enough.

How do we even begin to measure time when it comes to grief?

That hike to the beach I mentioned earlier....I went there. I cried there, practiced yoga, held my hands on my body and told her she was beautiful and that if it was right, we'd try again. I dreamed of the future, and made the decision to take a turn in my career path after this school year, to give myself more space.

I let myself journal and feel and weep and talk about it. Each time I chose my healing, I let the guilt fade more into the distance.

It was ok for me to prioritize myself.
It was ok for me to take the space I needed to heal.
It was ok to slow down.
It was ok.
It would be ok.
I would be ok.

And then, just a few months later, I was pregnant again - this time with my wildly creative and brilliant daughter.

One of my favorite places to hike with her is this same beach, where the ocean reminds us both that it's ok to take our time, to feel our feelings, and flow with more ease.

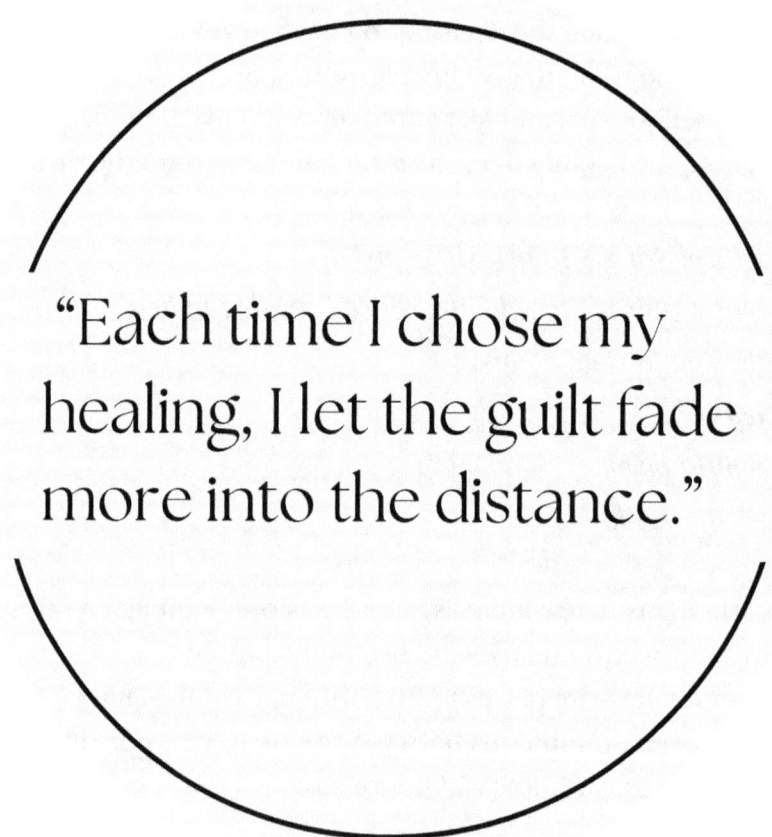

"Each time I chose my healing, I let the guilt fade more into the distance."

Exploring this chakra is an opportunity to get curious around your relationship to **flow, emotions, and the ability to create.** Are you able to access a sense of flow in your life and in your work? What conditions support your ability to experience joy, abundance and creativity?

My Reflections :

Your healing and relationship to the sacral chakra influences how you express yourself as a leader.

Applications to Your Leadership

THE SACRAL CHAKRA HELPS YOU LEAD BY...

- Honoring your one-on-one relationships, schedules and/or work protocols through supportive boundaries and emotional intelligence.

- Connecting to your creativity and intuition in your projects, visions and decisions.

- Finding energetic flow in your work and life, whether that means clear "work/life boundaries" or light structure in your day that is both flexible and supportive.

- Accepting change and transformation as a natural part of life, and understanding that it brings with it many emotions that can be worthy of examining.

On the following page, take some time to jot down any thoughts, reactions, sensations or emotions that are present in your experience **related to your leadership**. Note any ideas, connections or musings you want to remember before we think about specific moments where you and I both have chosen to Lead with Creativity.

My Reflections :

A Moment I Decided to Lead with Creativity

One of my favorite things about being an entrepreneur is the creativity that is required and that flows abundantly. When I'm consistently meeting my own needs and tuning into my desires, I can readily create and offer from a place of authenticity.

When I have a new idea for a workshop, I make it. I literally take it from the moment of inspiration to the announcement and launch, and there it is! Shiny and bright and new in the world.

The concept, the mission, and vision of my entire business was born from a place of creativity. From asking the question - what do I want to offer to the world? How do I want to be of service? And how do I want my days to look and feel?

There was a moment, walking around the lake near our home with my dear friend Kris, where she encouraged me to just do it. To start my own business offering leadership and wellness coaching. If I thought people needed it, they would find me.

I can picture us. Pausing mid walk, sun shining, encouraging each other to go after our hearts' deepest desires. The glimmer of excitement was growing in my body, and I knew then that I'd do it. I just needed that little bit of confirmation. I launched Lead and Be Well a quick three months later.

The flow that is required to create something from nothing is powerful!

I spent the next few months learning how to create a logo, build a website, start an LLC, and all the smaller steps along the way. I consulted with others who had gone a similar route, and I stayed deep in my yoga practice.

There was structure for sure. I need that structure to stay grounded, to show up for myself and this business I was creating, but there was also an ease. Almost a "getting out of my own way" to let the ideas come through. A commitment to holding the space, but letting go of needing to have it all figured out first.

It's quite like writing to you. I don't know exactly what I'll say until I sit down; I just let the words flow.

It's helpful to remember the feeling of these moments of Leading with Creativity. The ease, the abundance, the flow, the sense of being a channel. It can be a litmus test for other moments where the energy feels stagnant, stuck or leaky. A little light structure, some helpful boundaries aligned with purpose, and then the energy can flow freely once more.

One of Your Stories

- What do you want to say about the most defining one-on-one relationships in your life, and how they impact your ability to create as a leader in your life now?

- Write about a moment that you experienced a flow state. What were you doing? How did it feel? What structures or boundaries were in place to protect your energy? What emotions were present and how did they contribute to the moment? What conditions allowed you to access this state of flow?

- Think of a time either when you felt really balanced in this second chakra or this aspect of yourself. A time when you felt deserving of pleasure, in tune emotionally, and abundantly creative, clear on your boundaries (for yourself, your work, and/or in your life).

- Think of a moment that brought healing to the creative part of you. Have you had a time in your life where you introduced new boundaries that supported your ability to create and find flow in your life/work without guilt?

IT'S ALL CONNECTED

Embodiment Practices

The meditation and yoga can be practiced separately, or in either order. Experiment and see what feels most supportive in accessing a state of flow and abundance.

Meditation Script
(tap into creativity and flow)

Arrange your body in a comfortable position. Release any ideas about what this pose should look like, and choose one that allows you to really sink in and tune in to your breath. Once you are there, invite in some movements to allow yourself to get even more comfortable. Maybe circle the ankles and wrists, or bring gentle movements into the hips and shoulders.

Take a very deep breath in, fill the lungs all the way, then big sigh, release, let it all go. Now invite the breath to flow in and out naturally, without force. Trust that the body knows what to do, and lightly encourage it to have an evenness - an easeful flow in, and out.

Observe the breath. Notice how the breath comes in, and there's a peak, a sense of fullness, a wave cresting, before the breath naturally turns into an exhale, release, falling, a wave receding. Ride these waves of the breath a few rounds on your own.

Imagine yourself floating on these waves, perfectly supported by the most beautiful life raft or paddle board or sea creature - you decide. Let the body relax even more, but notice the subtle flow as the breath continues to rise and fall.

While you are resting, and floating here, imagine a scene of images floating in front of you, moments in time where you have been at your most creative. Maybe they are moments when you were a child, using your hands or your brilliant mind to bring forth new creations. Maybe they are moments growing up, expressing emotions, ideas, hope and dreams. Maybe these are recent moments - you as an adult, bringing forth creative energy into the world.

Notice how you feel. Track your body for any sensation or emotions. And come back to your breath, rising and falling.

The images in front of your eyes now shift to the future - images of you creating and being in flow. What do you see? What do you feel? What are you expressing? How are you Leading with Creativity? (pause and give time to notice what arises)

Take a very deep breath in, slowly exhale it out of the mouth. Hold on to any images, or thoughts, and begin to bring movement back into the body. Reach arms and legs in opposite directions, find your way to a seat. Grab your journal and write down/draw anything you'd like to remember from what you just experienced.

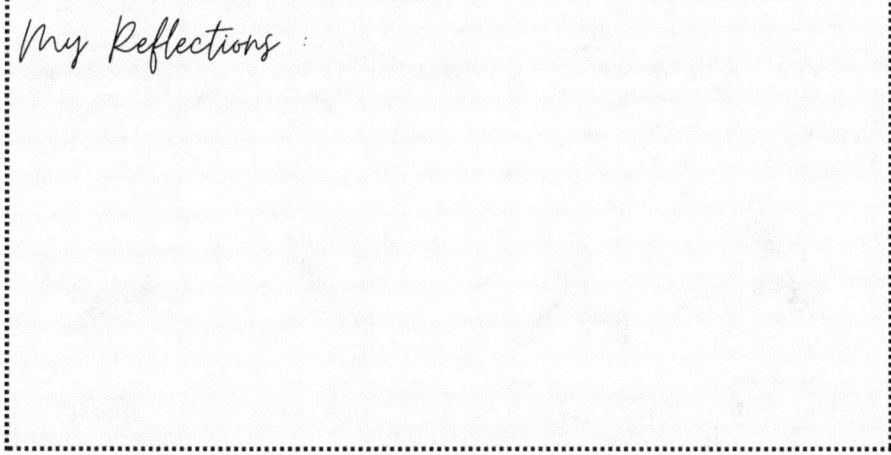

My Reflections :

Yoga Sequence

How to Practice

Throughout this creative flow, move seamlessly between the poses to help embody the water element. Feel your hips, your sacrum and stay connected through your low belly. Notice how one pose evolves naturally into the next.

Leading with Creativity is all about energetic flow, so consider how you could move in a way that allows you to express yourself. Allow this particular sequence to feel really pleasurable.

Warm up- Sun Salutation B

1 UPWARD MOUNTAIN → CHAIR

2 FORWARD FOLD → HALFWAY LIFT

3 PLANK → CHATURANGA

4 UPWARD FACING DOG

5 DOWNWARD FACING DOG

REPEAT 3X

6 WARRIOR 1 – R

7 PLANK → DOWNWARD FACING DOG

8 WARRIOR 2 – L

9 PLANK → DOWNWARD FACING DOG

10 MOUNTAIN ANJALI MUDRA

Flows

1A OPEN THREE-LEGGED DOG

1B WARRIOR TWO

1C REVERSE WARRIOR

1D EXTENDED SIDE ANGLE

RESET. REPEAT.

2A WARRIOR TWO   **2B** TRIANGLE   **2C** HALF MOON   **2D** STANDING SPLITS

RESET. REPEAT.

3A GODDESS   **3B** GODDESS TWIST   **3C** WIDE LEGGED FOLD   **3D** SIDE LUNGE

RESET. REPEAT.

4A LUNGE W/ HANDS INTERLACED   **4B** TWISTED LUNGE   **4C** HALF SPLITS   **4D** BRIDGE

RESET. REPEAT.

Cool Down

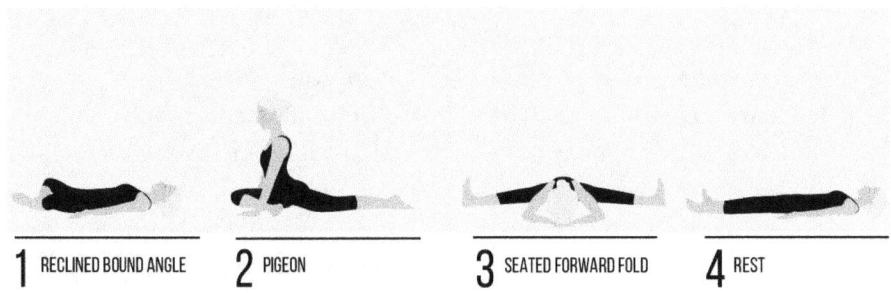

1 RECLINED BOUND ANGLE   **2** PIGEON   **3** SEATED FORWARD FOLD   **4** REST

how to engage with the theme of

CREATIVITY

body

- Move with flow and ease, like dance or yoga.
- Feel your hips as you sit, stand and change shape throughout your day.
- Listen to music and notice your body's response.
- Create a physical space that allows you to feel creative.
- Hydrate well.

mind

- Learn more about your birth story.
- Create art of any medium.
- Appreciate art created by others.
- Set and experiment with boundaries in your one-on-one relationships.
- Brainstorm or mindmap to find creative solutions to problems.

soul

- Let yourself cry.
- Visit a body of water and notice how you feel.
- Repeat your affirmations as if they were a song.
- Seek abundance, pleasure and joy in small moments.
- Journal about emotions - what they are, why you might be experiencing them, where it came from, and how it evolves.

work

- Create a fluid schedule to honor your energy changes.
- Practice flexibility in how/when/why things are created and accomplished.
- Honor energetic boundaries with colleagues.
- Notice moments in your day that you are actively creating.
- Give birth to new ideas, projects, conditions in your professional life.

Leading
with
CREATIVITY
means...

- Embodying the water element and tapping into your flow state.
- Remembering the impermanence, the state of change, and using this as a strength.
- Establishing strong boundaries, and loving one-on-one relationships.
- Using intuition and emotion as part of your decision making processes.
- Creating new visions, projects, ideas, and ways of being within yourself, your work, your family.
- Responding to life's inevitable changes with fluidity and calm.

PROMPTS FOR FURTHER REFLECTION

1. Choose an afternoon or full day this week to practice tuning into feeling your way from activity to activity without a set plan. Notice how it feels and write some reflections here.

2. Look through the lens of creativity this week - where might you be embodying creativity in unexpected ways?

3. Seek abundance this week. When you remember your definition of success, where can you see abundance already flowing freely in your life and leadership?

4. Consider how moving your body or sitting in stillness has impacted your connection to your leadership this week.

My Reflections :

_____

IT'S ALL CONNECTED

IT'S ALL CONNECTED

In Summary...

- Leading with Creativity correlates to the sacral chakra.

- Exploring, embodying and spending time reflecting on the water element can deepen your connection to this theme.

- Learning about, healing and loving your creativity, your one-on-one relationships, your desires, your passions, your worth, your emotions, your energy, and your boundaries is a way to balance this energy center. Invite in a flowing conversation to your present day life in ways that feel supportive to your growth.

- Exploring your creativity, what brings up guilt, and how to best feel in flow can be emotional - remember you deserve space here.

3 Lead with Confidence: "I Can"

"It is better to do one's own dharma, even though imperfectly, than to do another's dharma, even though perfectly."

~Bhagavad Ghita

Fueling Our Fire

There is an exciting quality when we speak of confidence, but notice if there is also a hesitation, a doubt as you read these words. The shadow present in this chapter is shame. A self doubt that asks, "who am I to take up this much space?"

This part of our journey is the place where I'll invite us to get curious about the Inner Critic and the Inner Best Friend. Our relationship to self-acceptance, self-criticism, self-esteem, and self-love.

The element associated with this leadership theme and energetic center is fire. It transforms, it digests, it activates and propels us forward. It brings people to us, drawing them to our warmth, our power, our brightness.

To Lead with Confidence is to give ourselves full permission to shine brightly. To take up space. To be who we are meant to be, and sing it from the rooftops. To walk our own walk, talk our own talk, and know that when we are grounded in our purpose, creating from our gifts, that we almost have no choice but to step confidently forward, trusting that our life, our leadership, our healing is of service in the world.

It's a time to practice connecting to our inner strength and power, and if that feels hard to access, revisit the first two themes and elements. Tap into grounding and your purpose. Feel into your ability to flow and create with ease. Remember who you are in relationship to the larger community, and what one-on-one relationships support your joy, abundance and creativity. From that support, breathe deeply into the gift that you are. Your unique perspective, life experiences, passions, dreams - this is the essence of this theme.

I hope you leave this chapter with a deeper confidence in who you are, knowing that you are connected to everyone and everything, AND you have a unique reason for being here. I hope you feel more ready to let yourself be seen.

What Does it Mean to Lead with Confidence?

Leading with Confidence is truly about remaining in your own power.

Picture Wonder Woman, the power stance, with hands on hips, heart open, spine tall, feet securely planted on the earth. A position that says, "I deserve to be here and I'm here to make an impact. I will not give my power away to doubt, to comparison, to shame. I will be my biggest cheerleader, my biggest hype person, and I'm going to get stuff done, one aligned action at a time."

When we Lead with Confidence, we have a sense of who we are

in so many ways. So we'll examine some of the internal voices and external structures that may influence our understanding of who we are.

Mini exercise #1:
Inner Critic & Inner Best Friend

These are the two voices that you likely hear all the time, maybe without even noticing them.

First, close your eyes and listen in to see if you can access your Inner Critic.

What does that voice say? Write it down, make a list and look at it objectively.

My Reflections :

Now, place one hand over your abdomen and one over your heart. Take a few deep breaths, and access your Inner Best Friend. This is the voice that speaks with confidence and love.

What does this voice say? Write it down.

My Reflections :

Read over the words from your Inner Best Friend, out loud, and notice how you feel. This voice reminds you to stand in your own power and let your light shine. This is the voice we want to access and amplify!

Using the Inner Best Friend voice, your most confident, wise and loving self, fill in the blanks to the phrase "I am a person who..." as many times as you want,

I am a person who...
I am a person who...
I am a person who...
I am a person who...

Bonus: Read your list out loud and let it be witnessed by someone you trust. Notice how you feel.

My Reflections : _____

_____

_____

_____

_____

_____

_____

_____

Mini exercise #2: Power, Privilege & Identity

Take a few breaths to settle into your body first, then reflect honestly on these questions:

- List some of your identity markers (some might include: race, socio-economic status, religious beliefs, physical and mental ability, gender and sexual orientation, level of education)
- Looking at this list, reflect on where you have more power and privilege? Where do you have less?
- Are there identities that feel very present in your lived experience and some that don't?
- How does that feel?
- How do these identities impact how you show in the world and in your leadership?

My Reflections : _____

_____

_____

_____

_____

_____

_____

_____

_____

IT'S ALL CONNECTED

Notice if shame arises in any area. It likely will. That's the shadow of the solar plexus chakra, and it's important to acknowledge it and work through it. Notice if anger arises as well. Consider the activation that anger can bring and how that feels like fire. It makes sense that in matters of unequal power, we feel both anger (*it should be different than this!*) and shame (*but I didn't mean to - is it my fault? Am I a bad person because of this?*)

I'll invite you to pause, and move your body, or even make some sound here. Shake, walk briskly, sigh deeply or yell. Discharge some energy.

My hope is that at this point, you have so much more context and clarity around who you are, what you value, what you are here to create, and how your unique life experiences all factor into WHO you are. Your unique soul.

Leading with Confidence is all about knowing who you are. Yes, in the context of the larger world, but also in the sacredness of your own being. When you feel energized to do your work, live out your purpose in the world, when you know that you are here to be a leader in a specific area - it's exciting! It's motivating! It helps us get up each day, ready to contribute, to take action, to say and do what's necessary to make a change in the world. To transform it. To do the things! To write the book, take the interview, ask the question, take the leap, say YES (or NO), try something out, start something new.

Let's learn more about this powerful energy center - the solar plexus chakra.

Name	Solar plexus chakra (manipura chakra)
Location in the body	Upper abdomen, stomach area
Parts of the body related to this chakra	Stomach, digestive system, metabolism, muscular system, pancreas, liver, gallbladder, spleen, and intestinal tract
Color	Yellow
Stone to work with	Amber, tiger's eye
Element	Fire
When this chakra is *balanced*, you feel...	• Self-confident, self-motivated • Empowered • Clear and aligned in your decisions • Resilient • Connected to inner strength
When this chakra is *out of balance*, you feel...	• Shameful or low self-esteem • Self-critical • Powerless or arrogant "power under or power over" • Unmotivated • Insecure

This chakra helps you *heal* **by...**	• Replacing shame with self-love and self-acceptance. • Re-establishing trust in your own worth, ability and power. • Creating a positive relationship to food, exercise, disordered eating or body dysmorphia. • Healing from oppressive or abusive situations/relationships
This chakra helps you *lead* **by...**	• Operating from a place of self-worth, self-confidence, self-esteem and self-acceptance. • Understanding your identity and how it shapes how you show up. • Articulating your current strengths, gifts, and growth areas. • Setting, working towards and achieving goals.
Shadow to explore	Shame
Affirmations	• I can. • I am confident. • I know who I am. • I trust the decisions I make. • I am resilient and brave. • I am capable. • I am empowered. • I shine bright.
Ways of being	Confident, trusting, decisive, self-assured. courageous

Feeling powerful? This information can feel really activating or make some want to run and hide. Invite some length into your spine and take a deep breath. Notice what it brought up in your body as you read through that list. Did you receive any insights from your body? Any images, sensations or urges come through? Stand tall and reflect on the idea that you are so capable and worthy of taking up space.

I invite you to take a minute and jot some notes down before jumping back in.

My Reflections :

Fire Element

The element associated with Leading with Confidence, and the solar plexus chakra, is FIRE. It is bright, warm, and powerful.

If you picture a campfire, or a raging wildfire - its power is undeniable. It can literally change the state of the wood, raw ingredients into nourishing meals, and the temperature of the air around you. When out of control, like in the case of the wildfires - it can destroy everything in its path.

The key to confidence is finding the right balance, where we are not giving our power away, or asserting our power over others. This element reminds us to harness the fire within us so that it sustains us, transforms us, without causing harm to those around us.

We can also think of the digestive fire within our gut, the system that transforms what we consume into nutrients and waste. Just like we need to balance our power in relationships, we need the right fuel to feel healthy in our literal bodies.[10]

Overloading our system with toxins or highly processed foods slows down the fire and we can feel sluggish. Not fueling enough leaves us feeling depleted and unable to take action.

I want to share a quote from one of my favorite Ayurvedic cookbooks, *Ayurveda Cooking for Beginners: An Ayurvedic Cookbook to Balance & Heal*. Ayurveda is the sister science to yoga and the connection to digestive wellness and our overall vitality is core to understanding the wisdom of Ayurveda. In the book, Plumb writes, "Tejas is inner radiance, the subtle energy of fire, through which we digest impressions and thoughts. It can be cultivated through contemplation, concentration, silence, studying nature and meditation. In the belly, tejas becomes agni, the power of fire to digest, metabolize, and transform. Agni is crucial to wellness, so supporting it is essential."[11]

Fire can be explained in an energetic sense as well. The energetic fire within us supports our ability to digest our experiences. Taking the time to process and make meaning from moments in your life allows those experiences to transform. You get to keep the wisdom, and release the waste.

It's about changing something.

As a leader - you are here to create some sort of change. Whether it's in our education system, our politics, our families, our environment, our relationships, or as individuals able to be present in our lives. It requires a lot of resilience. In yoga, we refer to this consistent effort as tapas, or the ability to stay in the fire of the practice. The consistent effort to show up each day and put one foot in front of the other.

As we show up, small moment to small moment, we build trust in ourselves - we build the confidence that we can and we will do the work. It increases our sense of self to be able to look back and say, "I did that! I was so brave/strong/loving/thoughtful/etc." The world needs this bright and shining version of you. It needs your wisdom and your courage to be able to stand up and share from your unique vantage point.

What have you learned that the world needs to hear? Where are you an expert, where once you were a beginner? Where have you put in the work, and built the trust within yourself? How can you use this to Lead with Confidence?

The impact of fire is powerful. Let the light of the flames remind you of your own inner power and confidence to create an evolving impact.

Fire

warm
active
initiating
strong
powerful
transformational
reminds us to shine

Pause & Process

At this point, you've taken in a lot of information! I'm going to invite you to pause and process for a moment. Use the space below to note five takeaways or write some questions that may be swirling around for you related to the theme of confidence.

An idea resonating with me is...

1

A question I have is...

2

I'm learning...

3

I'm wondering about...

4

A line of text that is sticking with me is...

5

Letting Our Light Shine Matters

I can still remember the first lesson I ever taught. I was 22, living in Mesa, Arizona, teaching a short math lesson to a group of eager fourth graders. I was nervous beforehand of course, but the minute I started speaking, I felt this sense of calm in my body. I was prepared, I was smiling, my purpose was so clear and allowed me to be focused on them.

I *was in the right place, doing the right work at the right time.*

I'm sure there were mistakes or areas to grow. Of course there were.

But I felt such a sense of knowing! This is what I'm meant to do! I'm good at this - not from a sense of ego, but just a truth. I'm a teacher.

Have you felt that before? Where were you? What were you doing?

I felt similarly when I transitioned into a leadership position many years later, and I felt it as a mom, first looking into Gabby's eyes.

This feeling - the full body YES - is the resonance I'm seeking when I want to Lead with Confidence.

When I was in that student teaching classroom, stepping into this new position of being their teacher, their leader, it wasn't about doing it perfectly. I didn't need to teach exactly like my mentor teacher either. She had her own style, and I learned an incredible amount of teaching wisdom from her, but we're different people.

I'm so grateful for her confidence in me - she encouraged me to teach like me, not like anyone else.

There's always been a slight difference between "Jess" and my "Ms. Plowman", or later, "Ms. Boots" personality, but not much. I chose to be me, teaching them math, or reading, or later on, teaching adults about criteria for success or strategic planning.

I felt most at home in my body, and most able to access a sense of confidence, when I cared about what I was sharing, knew my stuff because I was prepared, and trusted that I could read the room enough to adjust as needed.

The beautiful thing about confidence is that when we feel it, we want more of it! It deepens the sense of purpose, our ability to create, and our desire to do more of the actions that helped us feel confident in the first place.

For me, standing up in front of those sweet fourth graders, I was hooked. The identity of "teacher" firmly imprinted on my heart.

Applications to Your Healing

> **THE SOLAR PLEXUS CHAKRA HELPS YOU HEAL BY...**
>
> - Replacing shame with self-love and self-acceptance through empowering self talk and identifying moments of resilience.
>
> - Re-establishing trust in your own worth, ability and power through small daily actions and consistent follow through.
>
> - Creating a positive relationship to food, exercise, disordered eating or body dysmorphia.
>
> - Regaining confidence by being in trusting respectful relationships, and intentionally healing from past unhealthy or oppressive situations/relationships.

Take some time to jot down any thoughts, reactions, sensations or emotions that are present in your experience **related to your healing.** Notice anything that is coming up now that you might want to revisit later before we dive into exploring the shadow of this energetic center.

My Reflections :

Exploring the Shadow: Shame

I've experienced degrees of shame around my body for as long as I can remember. I was "too tall", and I remember cringing when family members would comment how "big" I was. They meant tall - I was an objectively thin child and young adult, but in the age of teen magazines, anything resembling "big" was the equivalent of "bad" in my mind.

Being the tallest in my class, I was always back row middle for any form of photo. I think I slouched a little all the way through high school, not wanting to be taller than the boys, "bigger" than the girls. The concept that girls should be "cute and little" is drilled into us in Disney movies, magazines and just about any TV show we raced home to watch after school.

In middle school, I fell into the pressure of experimenting with makeup, cool clothes, and restricted eating. You couldn't be thin enough, pretty enough, desirable enough. The comparison mental gymnastics were so real - and this was all before social media.

When we experience shame in the energetic part of the body related to power, it can lead to a desire to control what we can control.

This is partly why disordered eating or body dysmorphia shows up here - in the solar plexus chakra, in this chapter about confidence. If life feels out of control, or we are in situations where we feel like we don't have enough control...we reach for what IS in our grasp. For young women, that is often our bodies. What we do or do not feed it. How much or little we move it.

Without having any sort of diagnosis, I know I struggled with disordered eating for about a decade. Thoughts consumed with calories in and calories out. Wondering if I "earned" the food I was about to eat. Debating with myself if I had worked out hard or long enough to eat the necessary food for the day.

The tough reality - I don't know if I can name a close friend who *didn't* struggle with this in some form or another, at some time or another. It was healing to talk to each other, as our late 20's brought us free from that shame and into better relationships with our bodies.

Society praises certain ideals, and when this aspect of ourselves is seeking approval, connection, validation - it can be a dangerous feedback loop.

It takes so much strength to be with ourselves in any season, exactly as we are. To let shame melt away as we offer our bodies love, kind words, delicious food, rest, and movement because it feels good to move and for no other reason.

There are so many moments I can look back on and recognize that I was operating from a place of shame. Trying to please people. Trying to shapeshift to be worthy of a certain relationship or not. Trying to be something that I wasn't in order for someone to love me more.

Yoga was the path for healing that truly ended this cycle of shame for me. Yoga taught me to be in my body, appreciate my body, love my body, slow down and listen to my body, and be in relationship to it. Yoga taught me to burn away any shame and replace it with self love.

The studio I found when I moved to San Francisco introduced me to this incredible teacher - Stacie Overby- and her peaceful presence and message of "effort and ease" was the salve I needed. Week after week, I could feel my tension melting, my ability to be with myself in quiet moments lengthening, my awareness of my own self-talk and thought patterns deepening.

I cried in her class a lot. Typically in pigeon pose. Releasing years of old stories and self doubt. I learned how to take a softer version of a pose. I didn't need to always be striving, gripping, forcing. I could put my knees down in plank pose, and I was still worthy of being in her class. I could rest in child's pose, and I still deserved to be there.

If I could relax more into who I was and still belong here, where else would that be true?

Yoga literally helps my body stand taller.

It lengthens the muscles, creates more space in the spine. I practice standing taller, and taking up as much space as possible now every day. I hope and pray that this chapter allows you to do the same.

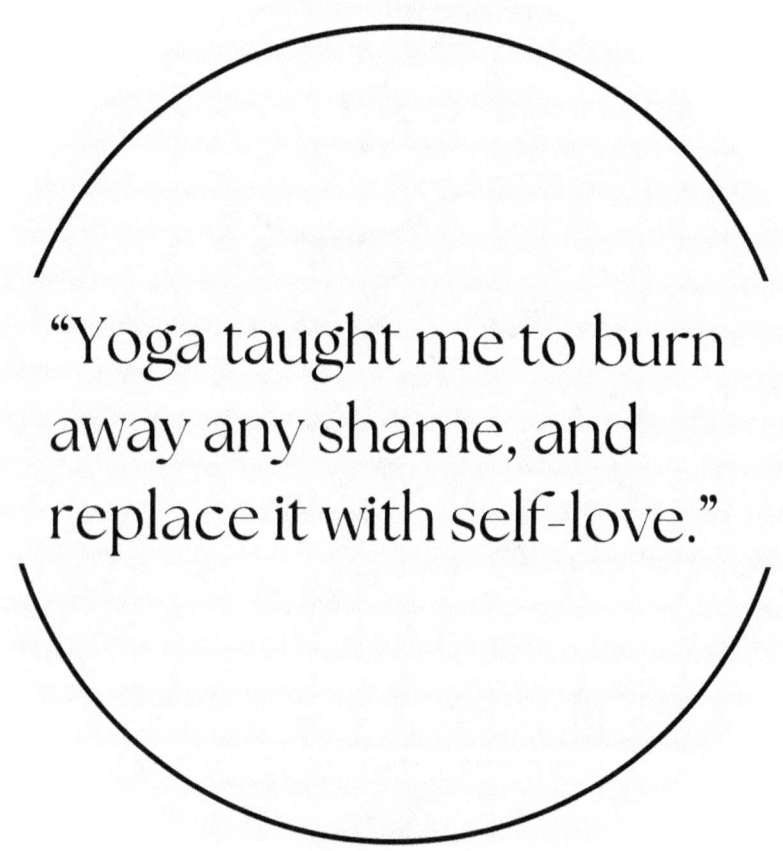

"Yoga taught me to burn away any shame, and replace it with self-love."

Exploring this chakra is an opportunity to get curious around your relationship to your **inner power, resilience and self worth.** Do you see yourself as the bright light that you are? What places, spaces or people support you in being your most authentic, confident self?

My Reflections :

All of this information impacts how you know and think about yourself as a leader.

Applications to Your Leadership

> ### THE SOLAR PLEXUS CHAKRA HELPS YOU LEAD BY...
>
> - Operating from a place of self-worth, self-confidence, self-esteem and self-acceptance so you can shine bright, and have clarity in your work.
>
> - Understanding your identity and how it shapes how you show up, especially in relation to naming and navigating power dynamics.
>
> - Articulating your current strengths, gifts, and growth areas. Knowing yourself well – what you value, who you are, how you make decisions, and what you are meant to do is essential to showing up as a leader.
>
> - Setting, working towards and achieving goals is central to building our confidence.

On the next page, take some time to jot down any thoughts, reactions, sensations or emotions that are present in your experience **related to your leadership**. Note any ideas, connections or musings you want to remember before we think about specific moments where you and I both have chosen to Lead with Confidence.

My Reflections :

A Moment I Decided to Lead with Confidence

When I was a sophomore in high school, I took a debate class. I remember nothing about the content of the debate, but I can picture the details of this room, the stadium seating, the podium centered on the stage.

The day before our first practice debate, I remember feeling nervous. Public speaking is the number one fear, right? When I shared this concern with my mother, she shook her head, claiming adamantly, "you are an amazing public speaker!"

I was? Oh well, great! That's good news.

My trust in her opinion was so strong, I took that vote of encouragement and ran with it. New identity formed.

I, Jessica, was an amazing public speaker. Nothing to fear.

And you know what? I crushed it.

I was prepared of course. I wrote my notes, practiced, and when my time came, I delivered with confidence. Clear voice, eye contact with a friend, no reading from my notes. This new belief naturally led to aligned confident action.

Looking back, I realize my mom was saying so much more than "I was going to be, no, already was, great at this particular skill".

It was a belief that I could be great at whatever I tried. Whatever I put my energy into.

It didn't matter that I hadn't done it before. All things are new to us at some point, and she believed, therefore so did I, that I could figure it out.

This shaped so much of my self-talk about what I could and could not accomplish in this life.

I've thought about this moment before the debate at many points in my life. When I've needed extra assurance, I remember how speaking that confidence into existence shined a light on the path forward.

I had no need to worry, I would find my way.

Thank goodness, because when I started Lead and Be Well, both my Inner Best Friend and my Inner Critic showed up with something to say.

Inner Bestie: "of course you can do this - anything you put your mind and heart to will work out. Go for it!"

Inner Critic: "who on earth do you think you are to start a business? Why would people work with you? What do you have to offer?"

Classic imposter syndrome.

The good news? My confident, Inner Best Friend voice is faster and louder, so I had already told people this business was happening, and we were off the races.

When you Lead with Confidence, you remember that you don't need to have it all figured out in order to begin.

One of Your Stories

- How has your relationship with yourself changed over the years? How does your self-confidence impact your ability to show up as a leader in your life now?

- What makes you, you? What unique skills, passions, experiences do you possess that make you uniquely you? How does it feel to speak about yourself?

- Think of a time either when you felt really balanced in this third chakra or this aspect of yourself. A time when you felt sure of yourself, empowered, confident in your goals and your ability to reach them. What were you doing? How did it feel? What strengths of yours were present?

- Think of a moment that brought healing to self-esteem or confidence. Have you had a time in your life where you released shame and stepped back into your self-love, power and acceptance? What does self-love look, sound and feel like to you?

IT'S ALL CONNECTED

Embodiment Practices

The meditation and yoga can be practiced separately, or in either order. Experiment and see what feels most supportive in activating some heat and transformation.

Meditation Script:

(tap into confidence and identity)

Find a comfortable seated or reclined position, and bring one hand to the solar plexus - the place above your navel, and the other to the low belly. Breathe into this space. Follow the breath for several rounds, letting the belly be soft and expand on the inhales, and contract on the exhalations. Give yourself permission to take up space here.

Now let your hands either stay here, or move to any part of the body that could use extra love and attention from you. Trust wherever they intuitively move. Breathe into this space. Follow the breath for several rounds, and maybe repeat the affirmation "I accept all parts of myself, exactly as I am", either in my heart or out loud.

Take a very deep breath in, open the mouth, let it go. Again, cleansing breath.

Finally, bring both hands to the solar plexus, above the belly button. Imagine a fire growing here. See and feel its heat. Watch as the flames dance and move with confidence. Imagine your breath growing deeper as you settle into this warmth of the fire - knowing that it is here to support you in shining brightly.

Imagine you see a log - and you know that this log represents some past experience. A moment that has helped transform you into who you are today. You know that when you toss this log into the fire, only the parts that fuel your highest good will remain. The rest will be burned away.

Now imagine tossing this log on to the fire, and watch it burn. Notice and feel the wisdom of that experience helping the fire shine even brighter, and the rest is gone, burned away. Let it go.

Wrapped in this warmth, take a moment to pause and notice how you feel.

Take a very deep breath in, fill the lungs, fill the belly, and then let it all go. Begin to move fingers and toes, reach arms and legs in opposite directions, and stretch. Find your way to a seat.

Pause and journal - what came up for you in this visualization?

My Reflections :

How to Practice

Throughout this fiery flow, feel and appreciate the heat as it builds in your body. Find your growth edge to help embody the fire element. Feel your core, the sides of the body, the twists, and stay connected to your strength.

Leading with Confidence is all about activation, so invite yourself to work hard, but sustainably in each posture. Allow this particular sequence to be empowering.

Warm up

REPEAT 3X

5 breaths here on each side...

1 DOWNWARD FACING DOG

2 PLANK

3 ONE-LEGGED PLANK LIFT R LEG / LIFT L LEG

4 COBRA

REPEAT 5X

5 LOCUST

6 DOWNWARD FACING DOG

7 FORWARD FOLD

8 MOUNTAIN ANJALI MUDRA

Flows

RESET. REPEAT.

1A CHAIR POSE

1B CHAIR W/ TWIST

1C FORWARD FOLD

1D HALFWAY LIFT

2A BOAT

2B FOREARM PLANK

2C SIDE PLANK--LEFT

2D SIDE PLANK--RIGHT

RESET. REPEAT.

REPEAT
3X

3A KNEE TO NOSE

3B HIGH LUNGE

3C WARRIOR 3
W/ ARMS EXTENDED

3D MOUNTAIN

RESET. REPEAT.

4A FOREARM PLANK
W/ SIDE DIPS

4B LOCUST W/ ARMS
REACHING FORWARD

4C LOCUST W/ ARMS
REACHING BACK

4D CHILD'S POSE

RESET. REPEAT.

Cool Down

1 SEATED SIDE BEND

2 SEATED TWIST

3 ONE-LEGGED SIDE BEND

4 REST

how to engage with the theme of

CONFIDENCE

body

- Activate fiery energy through core work and twists.
- Give your body time to fully digest its food.
- Build heat and sweat through vigorous exercise.
- Lift weights to strengthen your muscles.
- Work with a physical growth edge that feels exciting and invigorating.

mind

- Journal on all areas of expertise in your life.
- Reflect on challenges that you have overcome.
- Write a letter to a younger version of you about your current accomplishments.
- Call your bestie and take turns saying things you love about yourself!
- Visibly post motivating words from your Inner Best Friend.

soul

- Write the most empowering version of your day.
- Observe transformation taking place in nature.
- Repeat affirmations while looking in the mirror.
- Try something new that feels challenging and energizing.
- Say yes (and no) when you mean it.

work

- Celebrate your strengths at work.
- Leverage your strengths more in your professional life.
- Create a ritual where you regularly digest and process experiences at work.
- Refine your language to clearly convey your point.
- Explore dynamics of identity and power related to your career or role.

Leading
with
CONFIDENCE
means...

- Embodying the fire element to stand in your own power.
- Allowing things to transform so you can keep the wisdom, and release the waste.
- Having a connected, clear sense of self - owning your gifts, your strengths, and areas to grow.
- Knowing your capabilities, and trusting your ability to bring your vision into reality.
- Taking aligned action!
- Encouraging your light to shine brightly and impact those around you.

PROMPTS FOR FURTHER REFLECTION

1. Write down three good things and what you did to make these happen. How did that feel?

2. This week, listen for affirmations, validations, compliments, signs and words of what's going well being reflected back to you. What did you notice with that extra focus?

3. Who in your life do you allow close enough to see how brightly you shine? How does it feel to be around those people?

4. Consider how moving your body or sitting in stillness has impacted your connection to your leadership this week.

My Reflections : _____

_____

_____

_____

_____

_____

_____

_____

_____

_____

_____

_____

_____

_____

_____

_____

_____

_____

CONFIDENCE

In Summary...

- Leading with Confidence correlates to the solar plexus chakra.

- Exploring, embodying and spending time reflecting on the fire element can deepen your connection to this theme.

- Learning about, healing and loving your confidence, your relationship with yourself, your unique strengths, your talents, your resilience, your ability to transform, and your self esteem are all powerful ways to balance this energy center. Practice fueling your own fire with nourishing foods, experiences and opportunities.

- Exploring your confidence, what brings up shame, and how to shine brightly. This can surface energy that needs to be released - practice letting go in your own time here.

4 Lead with Love: "I Love"

"When we choose to be brave with our love - when we refuse to leave anyone outside our circle of care - our love becomes revolutionary."

~Valerie Kaur

Allowing for Spaciousness

Even as I sit to draft this chapter about love, I feel my eyes brimming with tears, and the telltale spread of warmth and tightness across my heart and throat. I'm not sure of an exact moment that is bringing this up, except that to write about love is to write about grief. And joy. And loss. And hope. And heartbreak. And loneliness. And connection.

How on earth do I choose words to represent the vastness of experiencing love?

As we explore this chapter about Leading with Love, we've reached the middle.

How beautiful is that? Of course love is in the middle. At the center.

There are the three preceding chapters, and the chakras are denser. There's a heaviness, a groundedness to the root, sacral, and solar plexus. We covered some intense topics. We dealt with fear, guilt, and shame. We explored what it means to Lead with Purpose and know where we belong. We inquired into our energetic flow and learned what boundaries support our ability to Lead with Creativity. We bravely claimed our individuality in order to Lead with Confidence.

And it brings us to love.

Breathe into that. Feel your lungs expand. The front, the back, the sides. Notice how good it feels to breathe deeply and create more space for air, more space for love.

The element we get to explore is of course, air, and we'll marvel at its abundance, reciprocal nature, and expansiveness.

We'll explore the shadow of grief, and you may notice how traces of grief were present in each other theme as well.

If you haven't yet noticed connections between the mind, body, soul and work and each theme to each other, I hope this chapter weaves those threads for you. I hope the connections between you and I get infinitely more clear. I pray the connections between your wellness and how you show up as a leader become incredibly obvious.

I hope you feel loved as you read.

What Does it Mean to Lead with Love?

When we Lead from Love, we have infinite reserves.

When our service is aligned with our love, when we allow ourselves to receive love as well as offer it out, we have enough. We remember we are enough. We are buoyed by this expansive, abundant quality of air. There's always more love to gain, more love to give.

When we approach our leadership from love, others feel that, and just as importantly, we feel that.

I do the work I do because I love it.

Because I love you.

Because I love my daughter and my husband.

Because I can't not do it.

When the work we do is aligned with purpose, it's in flow. When we take care of our energy, creativity is able to pour in. Our confidence in the meaning behind our work motivates us to take action. Then here we are... at love, and there's an expansiveness that lets the work take up space.

The love that we feel for life itself can be expressed as gratitude, but it feels like presence. It is expressed as that deep exhale into the present moment. Some awe and wonder mixed in - how incredible it is to be alive, to breathe and be here with each other. To feel and experience love and express it in different ways.

Mini exercise #1: Collecting Gratitude

This simple practice can be done anywhere, any time!

- Write down all the people, places and things that you love, and feel either gratitude or appreciation for.

- Write as many as you can, and when you're done, pause, read your list, and notice how you feel and where you experience sensations in the body.

- If you need to take a break, shift where you are (if you're inside, go outside, vice versa), look around and add to your list.

Gratitude List :

IT'S ALL CONNECTED

Do you feel warm across the chest, shoulders and down the arms? Are you smiling? Did you cry?

The word "love" can sometimes be relegated to romantic love; and some cultures have so many words for love. I personally feel that the more we use this word, with friends, with our family, with our experience of nature - the more we receive its warm glow.

Leading with Love reminds us that regardless of our work, we are first and foremost humans, having a human experience. The spaciousness of air encourages us to keep in perspective that we are not machines clocking in and out. Everyone has their own story, their own purpose, their own grief that they carry with them. Yes, even the person honking in traffic. Or the politician saying hateful things. Even them.

So as leaders, when we remember to Lead with Love, we expand our capacity to understand the details of a moment. Rather than taking the narrow view, we broaden the narrative. We ask questions. We get curious about what else might be true before we take action.

What might be the most generous version of this scenario?

If I assumed everyone is doing the best they can given the tools available to them, what might shift in how I approach this conversation, this project, this perceived problem?

If I considered who needs extra love and support right now, where might I direct my energy?

If I paused, took a breath, and accessed love - how might things play out differently?

Mini exercise #2:
Writing Love Letters

The act of writing is so powerful. It helps us heal. Take all the time you need, but you might also engage with these letters in a way that feels light. You decide.

- Write a love letter to yourself at any age, past, present or future.
- Write a love letter to someone who you love with ease.
- Write a love letter to someone who is much harder for you to love - but write from your soul to their soul.

My Reflections : _____

_____

_____

_____

_____

_____

_____

_____

_____

_____

_____

_____

_____

_____

_____

_____

_____

_____

_____

_____

_____

_____

_____

_____

_____

_____

_____

How was that? What emotions were present? Take some time to note any reflections on how your understanding of Leading with Love is adjusting.

If you are ready to expand your understanding of love, let's learn more about the heart chakra, tell some stories and talk about Leading with Love.

Name	**Heart chakra (anahata chakra)**
Location in the body	Center of the chest
Parts of the body related to this chakra	Chest, lungs, heart, shoulders, arms, hands, fingers, respiratory system
Color	Green
Stone to work with	Pink rose quartz, aventurine
Element	Air
When this chakra is *balanced*, you feel...	• Compassionate for self and others • Gracious • Generous • Joyful and peaceful • Nourished when caring for others
When this chakra is *out of balance*, you feel...	• Lonely or antisocial • Resentful or bitter • Lacking in compassion • Disconnected • Depleted by caring for others

This chakra helps you *heal* **by...**	• Moving through grief related to experiences of loss (death, abandonment, or separation, rejection). • Forgiving yourself and others. • Practicing loving kindness towards all Beings. • Noticing areas of life where you struggle to give or receive love and get curious about these.
This chakra helps you *lead* **by...**	• Loving people, even when you disagree with them. • Making decisions with empathy and considering others' feelings. • Giving generously of your time, energy, & efforts without depleting your own reserves. • Modeling and offering opportunities for vulnerability.
Shadow to explore	Grief
Affirmations	• I love. • I am love. • I offer. • I receive. • I am compassionate. • I empathize. • I forgive. • I breathe.
Ways of being	Compassionate, forgiving, generous, vulnerable, empathetic

Invite in a long, slow breath. Gently release it. Notice what it brought up in your body as you read through that list. Did you receive any insights from your body? Did any people, places or things that you love, or maybe have lost, come to your awareness as you took in that information? Pause for a moment to really sit with the idea that at the center of it all, is love.

I invite you to take a minute and jot some notes down before jumping back in.

My Reflections :

Air Element

The element associated with Leading with Love, and the heart chakra is AIR. It's expansive, spacious and light.

The element of air reminds us to be *in relationship.*

Inhale , exhale.

Fill up , release.

Receive , offer.

Think of the trees and plants on our planet. All day every day, we exhale carbon dioxide, which would be poisonous for us to breathe, and the trees gratefully use that carbon dioxide to sustain their lives. In return, they release the necessary oxygen we require to survive. Some trees even look like lungs![12]

The expansive element of air reminds us to keep it simple. Most mindfulness or meditation practices begin with breath awareness. We practice narrowing the scope of attention and sensation to a single breath as it enters, fills and leaves the body. Through repetition, we begin to focus the mind, calm the nervous system and feel more peaceful and present. In *The Illuminated Breath*, a comprehensive study on the science of ancient yoga breath practice, Dylan Werner writes, "Pranayama (breathwork) is a practice of conscious breathing whereby we change the depth, rate, rhythm, and quality of each breath to move toward an intention."[13] This tool, the breath, is a free and abundant resource for most people. Always available, always accessible.

So is love. Love is abundant, it is available and yet sometimes we close ourselves off. There is a vulnerability to breathing deeply, to opening ourselves up to love and be loved. It can feel too dangerous to be exposed in that way.

Breathing with intention and depth reminds us we don't need to do it all at once. We can, and often need to, take things one breath at a time. It would be impossible to take in all the oxygen we need in a lifetime. That's not how it works. We breathe in just once, then we have to let it go. Making space is required in order to take in more. There is no rush. There's time and space to move at your own pace.

Maybe even try it right now. Pause and take in a full breath. Pause and notice what it feels like. Then slowly, release all of it, really exhale completely. Then breathe in again. There is room, space, opportunity to take in new air.

If you compare this to love or generosity, put simply, the more we offer away, the more we are bound to receive. If you were to give so much love away, create so many connections, offer your heart your vulnerability, your gifts with the world, you are likely to receive just as much. Those connections, they turn around and fill you up.

How we work with the air element can be so simple. Notice yourself breathe as much as you can throughout your day. Create more space between activities. Breathing room, right?

And next time you go for a walk by trees, contemplate the intimate relationship occurring, and maybe pause to say thank you.

Air

spacious
expansive
light
abundant
relational
essential
reminds us to balance offering and receiving

Pause & Process

At this point, you've taken in a lot of information! I'm going to invite you to pause and process for a moment. Use the space below to note five takeaways or write some questions that may be swirling around for you related to the theme of love.

An idea resonating with me is...

1

A question I have is...

2

I'm learning...

3

I'm wondering about...

4

A line of text that is sticking with me is...

5

Air & Water...a Connection

As I initially wrote about grief, the shadow of the heart chakra, I noticed something interesting. All the words I used to describe grief were not about air...but water.

Grief - the gaping hole, the rushing river, the deepest well of emotion.

Sometimes I fear that when I allow myself to experience grief - like for real, I will be swallowed by it.

Do you ever feel that way? Like you'll open the gates and get washed away.

I definitely feel this concern. But, I've opened the gates. I've felt the waves of grief wash over me. Sometimes I've been knocked down. I can picture moments in the shower - sitting on the floor crying. But instead of getting washed away, I end up feeling cleansed. And then I close the gates, and know I'll open them a little more later.

The metaphors I naturally use for grief all have to do with water....even though the element for the heart chakra is air.

Why is that?

I think it's because grief is so connected to the second chakra. The one-on-one relationships we have....when we lose someone dear to us, this is usually the deepest type of grief. And that's our water, the one-on-one relationships we have in our lives are part of the theme of the sacral chakra.

Maybe we need the spaciousness of air to breathe deep enough to let the water flow. Maybe we need the buoyancy, the life raft if you will, of air to float in that river. To remind us of our resiliency, our ability to float, to swim, to navigate. Air reminds us to access ease so we can relax on that floaty instead of swimming upstream trying to escape.

My Reflections :

Your Healing & Leadership: Application of "Leading with Love"

Expanding Our Capacity to Love Matters

My meditation practice found me in a season of life where I was finally ready - desperately so - to slow down a little, and acknowledge what my heart was trying to tell me.

Even though there were a few moments of meditation always attached to yoga classes, I fidgeted through them, or counted the moments in savasana until it was time to go. I didn't realize it, but my body and my mind were fighting so hard to keep up some armor around my heart, safeguarding the grief that lived inside.

I remember my first love, all the way back in college, was seeking a depth from me that I couldn't yet give. That was frustrating for us both, I'm sure. For me, I can see now that I just wasn't ready to do the work of healing. I wasn't ready to acknowledge the loss I endured as a child, and feel that pain, beyond the surface level, story-telling version. I wasn't able to articulate how that loss made vulnerability challenging for me, how it embedded a fear of being worthy of love into all of my relationships. I didn't yet have the strength to say, "if I share this part of me, will you still love me?" I wasn't ready to open the conversation of what it means to truly love and be loved - in our entirety.

Sitting in silence with myself was the doorway in. It still is.

A friend and former colleague of mine, Adam, offered mindfulness for our students, and began to offer moments of mindfulness for the staff as well. Sometimes just five minutes before we went out to crosswalk duty.

Sitting in the quiet room, being invited to notice my breath, and *allow* whatever I was feeling to come through...oh wow, the tears flowed immediately. Which, logistically, was tough timing since I needed to then go outside and greet middle-schoolers. But the message was clear:

I need more of this.
There's something here.
Slow down. Listen. Pay attention.

I began experimenting with quiet moments at home, allowing for the softening to take place in my yoga classes. I picked up my journaling practice again - my old companion that has followed me since I learned to write.

I learned how to sit with myself.

I know now that my body was releasing tension, stress that accumulated during the day and throughout my lifetime. Through slowing down, I was shifting from the sympathetic nervous system to the parasympathetic nervous system, from fight or flight mode to rest and digest mode. My body needed it so badly that it didn't take much to activate tears and a sense of release.

It was a slow shedding of layers - self-protection, fear of vulnerability and that fear of being swallowed by grief if I gave it permission to be present. I learned that I could acknowledge grief, feel it, and then let some of it go. I learned that I could feel lighter as a result. I learned I don't have to carry it all around with me forever. It's part of my story, but that doesn't mean it has to define me or weigh down my heart.

I learned to love myself. That I was not unworthy. Unlovable. I didn't need to strive so hard to be put together or seem perfect. But in fact, quite the opposite. I could relax a little. That I was, just like you are, worthy and made of love exactly as I am. If I dropped the ball, I could pick it back up. No worries.

As my self-compassion grew, my compassion for others did as well.

That's how love works. The more we see, hear, tend to, make

space for, and love on the parts of ourselves we once believed we needed to hide, the more capacity we have to see and love those parts in others as well.

My meditation practice continues to be the place I go to access self-compassion, clarity, peace, and wisdom.

I understand now not to fear diving into grief, because at the bottom of it, on the sides of it, swirled into it, is love.

Applications to Your Healing

THE HEART CHAKRA HELPS YOU HEAL BY...
• Moving through grief related to experiences of loss (death, abandonment, or separation, rejection). Give yourself all the space and time you need. • Forgiving yourself and others. Lightening the emotional load that you carry can help you be more available for what is present in your life right now. • Practicing Loving-Kindness towards all Beings. Self-compassion practices increase our ability to extend compassion to others. • Noticing areas of life where you struggle to give or receive love and get curious about these.

Take some time to jot down any thoughts, reactions, sensations or emotions that are present in your experience **related to your healing**. Notice anything that is coming up now that you might want to revisit later before we dive into exploring the shadow of this energetic center.

My Reflections :

Exploring the Shadow: Grief

There was a Friday recently where I was reflecting on my coaching sessions. It was a full day, five clients, with short breaks in between. I had a moment where I noticed that there were tears present in every single session. That isn't always the case, but it's also not unusual. These powerful leaders - many of whom are moms in addition to being leaders in their schools - experience personal and tangential grief all the time. They hold a lot of pressure to perform, accomplish, and a never-ending list of things to take care of. Which can sometimes feel like grief of personal freedom.

Some days they - I - we have enough space to process it all on their own, and some of the time, we wait until someone who deeply cares about us asks, "how are you? Like, the real version?" and we have the opportunity to take a deep breath, and answer honestly about what feels hard.

Grief is often present in coaching conversations, because we're humans, who are constantly moving through change. Sometimes when we hear the word grief we think of big T trauma. Loss of a parent or experiencing a type of abuse. But grief can happen in smaller moments as well. When things shift from being one way to being another.

There's a subtle form that's always present when things end - these are often mingled with joy, so it can be confusing. Graduations, staff members leaving, moving to a new town, your baby growing older, completing a project, roles adjusting within our building or families. This grief is dancing with anxiety and excitement and anticipation and pride and uncertainty and hope. It can be overwhelming, which I believe is why words are often hard to grasp, so we hug and cry instead.

Grief can be almost a little contagious. Consuming the news, social media, hearing from a close friend about their sad news...it's a lot to take in. We know we are connected to one another, and so when we see others in pain, we often feel that pain as well.

Here's the thing. No matter the size of the grief - it deserves being seen.

The best way I've found to work through emotions - especially grief - is to first name them. Acknowledge that they are here with us in the conversation. By allowing those emotions, and giving them some space to breathe, they can loosen the hold they have on us a little. They can be processed and released.

Sometimes we can move through the grief by talking, or by moving our bodies, or connecting with the breath.

A walking coaching session can do wonders for feeling calm and grounded, getting back into the body, and releasing what you don't need to hold on to anymore.

It is such a gift to offer people time and space to speak what's on their hearts, in an unfiltered, unhurried way. Often the practice starts with offering ourselves that spaciousness. To sit with our own feelings, to listen to what our heart is longing for. To grab our journal and pour our dreams and desires and grief on the waiting pages.

Processing grief on a regular basis allows us to witness the world with a deep sense of gratitude. When we give ourselves this space, we can more quickly shift to remembering all the abundance around us, each new day in front of us, and where we can take empowered action.

As leaders, when we learn that our big emotions are temporary and can be released, we can sit with others going through tough moments as well. We can hold a spacious container for them to learn and unpack theirs in their own time.

Leading with Love sounds like, "Can I be here, in this moment with you, one breath at a time, not needing the moment to be anything other than it is?" That feels like love.

The ever-presence of grief is not meant to swallow us. It's a reminder to be kind to others. Everyone's holding more than we imagine.

I believe it's a reminder to go back to the beginning. To Leading with Purpose. To ground in the energy of earth, to remember how we want to be of service in the world and then take inspired action. It's just one way that these themes are all connected. We need the steadiness of earth to remind us that we are in fact ok. We need the permission of water to feel and create. We need the activation of fire to go take action and contribute to good in the world, and love reminds us to practice compassion towards ourselves and each other. When you thrive, I thrive. When you suffer, I suffer. Let us love each other along the way.

"Processing grief on a regular basis allows us to witness the world with a deep sense of gratitude."

Exploring this chakra is an opportunity to get curious around your relationship to **love, generosity, and gratitude.** Are you able to balance giving and receiving in your personal and professional relationships? What conditions support your ability to experience a sense of lightness and spaciousness in your heart?

My Reflections :

All of this information influences how you appreciate yourself as a leader.

Applications to Your Leadership

THE HEART CHAKRA HELPS YOU LEAD BY...

- Loving people, even when you disagree with them. Expansive love is so much bigger than the small likes and dislikes, even than the difference of values. We can love the soul, and disagree or stop harm when it's being done.

- Making decisions with empathy and considering others' feelings. It might take more time, but will usually need less follow up afterward.

- Giving generously of your time, energy, and efforts without depleting your own reserves.

- Modeling and offering opportunities for vulnerability whether in your family, your place of work, or with yourself.

On the following page, take some time to jot down any thoughts, reactions, sensations or emotions that are present in your experience **related to your leadership.** Note any ideas, connections or musings you want to remember before we think about specific moments where you and I both have chosen to Lead with Love.

My Reflections :

A Moment I Decided to Lead with Love

I drive my daughter to school most mornings. Sometimes we listen to music, or sing or chat about the day ahead. Some days, she is cranky. Some days, I am cranky.

Some days, we talk about love.

One especially sweet morning I was driving my daughter to preschool. As I buckled her in she said, "mama, I love you 8 billion, 5 trillion, 42 89...etc. etc." (I'm sure I'm misrepresenting the number, but you get the point. It's a lot.)

It's a game she loves to play. She tries to create the biggest number she can imagine, and then I do the same. She always says her number is bigger than mine. I always say it's a tie. Sometimes we do it with distance, "to Jupiter and back! No, to Pluto and back!"

On this particular morning, she added, "That's how much I love you and Dada. I love all the people I love the same amount. Otherwise, it's not kind."

And so we talked about how amazing it is that we never run out of love.

That there is always enough. That when we meet a new person, and we have love for them, we just get more love to give. We don't have to take it from anyone else. More just appears. And how it's sort of like magic.

In fact, the more love we use, the more love we have.

What else is like that in the world?

It's the biggest lesson in abundance.

Our minds can easily default to scarcity when we experience fear, or loss, or grief. We can tend to close up, to cling tightly, to act as if we'll run out.

This conversation with Gabrielle helped me stay grounded in the truth about Leading with Love in our work, in our families and in our lives.

Love reminds us that when we stay open, when we freely give

and receive love, we have more than enough. We have an endless supply.

In my coaching work, I Lead with Love all the time. Through encouraging someone to take our coaching meeting outside on a walk, leaning in to listen more deeply, offering a hug, nodding my head, guiding them back to their wisest and most compassionate self, telling them they are an incredible leader, ending virtual sessions with an air hug, laughing or crying alongside as they share their joys, challenges and celebrations. They are all expressions of love that make their day better...and mine as well.

One of my favorite mindsets from coaching training is the premise that "the client is already whole". My job as a coach is to help hold that vision for them, reflect back their wholeness. I can practice this in my leadership at work, but also with my family and friends. When I hold and share this most generous version of who they are, I invite them to envision it themselves.

One of Your Stories

- What do you want to say about your ability to give and receive love? How does it impact your current relationships as a leader?

- Write a story about spaciousness. When and where do you experience enough room to breathe in your work or your relationships and what's the impact?

- Think of a time you felt balanced in this fourth chakra or this aspect of yourself. A time you were able to show up with compassion, for yourself or someone else, or a time you felt generous, empathetic, loving and kind.

- Think of a time you healed something in your heart - is there a story about unresolved grief that wants to be told? Write this story with love. Notice how it may or may not intertwine with other themes or chakras.

IT'S ALL CONNECTED

Embodiment Practices

The meditation and yoga can be practiced separately, or in either order. Experiment and see what feels most supportive in expanding your capacity for love.

Meditation Script:
(tap into love and compassion)

Find a comfortable place to sit or lay down. Encourage length in the spine and spaciousness across the heart. When you feel settled in the body, turn your awareness to your breath.

Get curious around the place where the breath enters the body. Start with the beginning of the breath. For the next few rounds of breath, give all your attention here, the place where the breath initiates.

Then notice how the breath fills the lungs, the expansiveness you feel and where you feel it. For several rounds, focus your awareness here, the sensation of fullness.

Finally, notice the exhale. The natural process of the air leaving the body. You might notice the lower lobes of the lungs contracting and gently squeezing all the air out of the body. For a few rounds of breath, pay attention to the release, the exhale.

Now, let the breath find a natural rhythm, without much of our attention. You might bring one hand or both hands over your heart, and cultivate some feelings of warmth, kindness and love for yourself.

Repeat out loud or in your heart, *May I be safe. May I be healthy. May I be happy. May I be at ease.* Repeat 2 more times.

Now call to your heart mind someone you love so much - maybe someone who you know could use a little extra love and compassion today. Repeat out loud or in your heart. *May you be safe. May you be healthy. May you be happy. May you be at ease.*

Lastly, we'll call to mind a large community, the whole world if you can, wrap your loving, kind energy around them. And repeat out loud or in your heart. *May you be safe. May you be healthy. May you be happy. May you be at ease.*

Take a very deep breath in, gently exhale it out. Bring movement into the body, take a big stretch. Come on up to a seat, Grab your journal and reflect on anything that came up for you in that practice.

My Reflections :

How to Practice

Throughout this heart-centered flow, move spaciously between the poses to help embody the air element. Feel your heart, your lungs, your shoulders and connect through your arms and hands.

Leading with Love is all about viewing your heart as a true center. Use the inhales and exhales to expand and contract each posture to create a rhythm for your practice. Allow this particular sequence to be expansive.

Warm up

REPEAT 5X

1 CAT → COW FLOW

2 DOWN DOG

3 MOUNTAIN ANJALI MUDRA

4 MOUNTAIN UPWARD SALUTE

REPEAT 3X

5 FORWARD FOLD

6 HALFWAY LIFT

7 COBRA

8 DOWNWARD DOG

Flows

1A STANDING SIDE STRETCH R --> L

1B FORWARD FOLD W/ TWIST

1C CHAIR

1D CHAIR TWIST

RESET. REPEAT.

2A HIGH LUNGE

2B LUNGE W/ HANDS INTERLACED

5 breaths here...

2C PLANK

2D SIDE PLANK

RESET. REPEAT.

3A WARRIOR ONE

3B WARRIOR TWO

5 breaths here...

3C PLANK

3D WILD THING

RESET. REPEAT.

REPEAT 5X

4A FOREARM PLANK / SPHINX FLOW

4B LOCUST

4C BOW

4D CHILD'S POSE

RESET. REPEAT.

Cool Down

1 BRIDGE

2 RECLINED BOUND ANGLE

3 SUPINE TWIST

4 REST

how to engage with the theme of

LOVE

body

- Hug someone or a tree.
- Relax into restorative heart-opening yoga poses.
- Feel the shoulders, chest, back and hands as you move throughout your day.
- Practice different forms of breathwork and observe the impact of each.
- Hike a mountain and notice the air and the trees as you breathe.

mind

- Begin or practice seated meditation - simply observing the breath.
- Name five things you are grateful at close of day.
- Place your hands over your heart and repeat affirmations.
- Practice a loving-kindness meditation.
- Pay attention to your self-talk and choose loving language.

soul

- Express love to yourself, your friends, and your family.
- Share and receive Reiki healing energy.
- Journal freely about people, things, and moments that help you access love and gratitude.
- Write a letter of forgiveness (maybe send it, maybe not).
- Connect with your grief and create a healing ritual around what you are grieving.

work

- Write notes or cards expressing appreciation for colleagues.
- Allow time for people to express gratitude and love for one another.
- Begin meetings with a few present breaths.
- Assume the most generous interpretation of an event.
- Practice compassion for self and others as you grow.

Leading
with
LOVE
means...

- Embodying the quality of AIR to remember to let things breathe.
- Seeing the highest good, the most generous version of and for each other.
- Practicing vulnerability and empathy.
- Acknowledging that grief is present when change is present.
- Working for the benefit of all Beings.
- Believing that everyone is worthy of, capable of, and deserves love.

PROMPTS FOR FURTHER REFLECTION

1. What is one thing you could do this week that would feel really self-loving?

2. Who is someone in your life that you could offer or receive more love to/from? What would shift if you allowed that love to flow more freely?

3. If you let love guide your leadership decisions this week, what would that look like? Sound like? Feel like?

4. Consider how moving your body or sitting in stillness has impacted your connection to your leadership this week.

My Reflections :

_____

_____

_____

_____

_____

_____

_____

_____

_____

_____

_____

_____

_____

_____

_____

_____

_____

_____

_____

My Reflections : _____

_____

_____

_____

_____

_____

_____

_____

_____

_____

_____

_____

_____

_____

_____

_____

_____

_____

_____

_____

_____

L O V E

In Summary...

- Leading with Love correlates to the heart chakra.

- Exploring, embodying and spending time reflecting on the air element can deepen your connection to this theme.

- Learning about, healing and loving your ability to give, receive and be loved is center to your growth! Practice appreciation, gratitude, empathy and compassion for yourself, others and the planet to balance this energy center.

- Leaning into our love, acknowledging grief, and contemplating how we are all connected are at the center of our experience. Give yourself lots of space to breathe here.

5 Lead with Truth: "I Speak"

"True power comes from standing in your own truth and walking your own path."

~Liz Gilbert

Listening for Resonance

In the journey of learning a new language, the first step is always listening. We must learn to listen before we speak. The more tangible forms of communication, like reading and writing, come later.

When we slow down and practice deep listening - both within ourselves and to others - we can be more discerning with the words we decide to share with the world.

As you read through this chapter, there might be moments from your past that emerge. Times you were told to either stay quiet, take up less space, or the opposite. Someone may have told you to, "be brave, just say it, use your words."

The work of the previous themes all have the opportunity to show up here.

Can we speak our purpose with confidence?

How do our creative expressions resonate with others?

How can we communicate the truth of who we are, with love, to ourselves and the world?

As we dive in, this is a beautiful time to listen for resonance. Which of my words feel like truth to you? What strikes a chord deep within you, and which ones challenge you?

The element we'll explore is sound, and I hope that as a result, you find yourself hearing more clearly.

I'll share stories of when I needed to speak up, and others when I learned to listen. Like all chakras, it's about both. To be a leader, it's imperative that we can do both. When we give ourselves enough time and space to listen inward, to hear the thoughts and opinions of others, we are more able to then choose the words that communicate truth and love and wisdom.

The shadow to explore here is lies - both the ones we tell others and the ones we tell ourselves, regardless of the size. It's time to practice honesty.

What Does it Mean to Lead with Truth?

Leading with Truth is all about communicating in a way that feels honest, aligned, heartfelt and authentic.

Imagine all the work you've done to get grounded in your purpose and in your own creative desires is swirling upward in your body. It gets activated and confidently clarified as it moves through your unique experience and deeply felt with love. This energy, this message, this offering, then is able to come forth through your words.

The words you speak, sing, write, recite, offer, shout, whisper and chant into the world.

What is it that you want to share that is full of truth and love?

There is a lot of noise out there, conflicting messages, busy advertising, and it can be literally hard to hear one another sometimes.

Considering what message we have to share in the world is part of our work here.

Mini exercise #1:
Message of Truth

Imagine that you had a room full of people, ready to hear you speak. This was the only time you had their full attention, and you want to leave a lasting impact, but only have a few minutes to share.

What truth would you offer to them? Take time to really imagine, hear and see the response.

My Reflections :

Whatever words, emotions, images, songs come through - write it down! This is the essence of your truth. Is it aligned with your purpose? Does it change or slightly shift what you originally thought to be your purpose?

My Reflections :

_____

_____

_____

_____

_____

_____

_____

_____

_____

_____

_____

_____

_____

_____

_____

Here, again, we remember that *it's all connected.* If you notice a difference between what you originally thought your purpose was and the truth that wants to be shared with the world...what do we do with that?

Use the body. Turn inward. Get quiet with yourself, and find where the alignment exists and where the energy gets stuck.

Notice where the throat constricts and where the words pour out. Where the breath flows smoothly. In what conditions do you feel at home in your body, or pleasantly at your growth edge? What resonates deeply and echoes in your heart?

Tune into your gut and your ability to share with confidence.

Don't let the details on how you share get in the way. Sharing our truth with one person or a whole room - this is not the point. The point is, what is your unique perspective? What is the truth, from your seat, from your life's vantage point?

As a leader, there are bound to be people listening to your words. You may find moments where you speak imperfectly. Of course you will. It's always imperfect. There are clues in this journey. What is it you wished you had said? What parts felt right? What resonated with others? What came through that you hadn't planned but felt exactly true as you spoke it.

Sometimes the most powerful words are the hardest to say:

> *I love you.*
> *I need help.*
> *I'm sorry.*
> *I forgive you.*
> *Will you forgive me?*

The shadows from the previous chapters can sneak in and block these words. Maybe we're afraid. Maybe we feel we don't deserve it. Maybe we're ashamed or still grieving.

The inability to speak certain phrases gives us clues about where we need more healing. The words unspoken can be a heavy weight to carry, and the lightness that follows when we finally say them... an unimaginable relief.

Mini exercise #2:
Say the Unsaid

Consider a relationship or situation where you intuitively know there are words unspoken. Either from you or from others. Imagine you could clear all blockages and let the words flow.

Either practice this conversation aloud or write it out.

Notice what comes up.

My Reflections :

How did that feel? What energy was released? If that brings up a lot, give yourself some space and take care of yourself.

My Reflections :

_____

_____

_____

_____

_____

_____

_____

_____

_____

_____

_____

_____

_____

_____

_____

When you are ready, let's explore some information about the throat chakra and what we can learn from it.

Name	**Throat chakra (vishuda chakra)**
Location in the body	Throat, neck
Parts of the body related to this chakra	Throat, mouth, lips, teeth, tongue, and neck
Color	Light blue, turquoise
Stone to work with	Lapis lazuli, blue lace agate
Element	Sound
When this chakra is *balanced*, you feel...	• Honest • Fluent with listening and sharing • Expressive with words and thoughts • Able to advocate for self and others • Aligned with supportive ideas
When this chakra is *out of balance*, you feel...	• Drawn towards lying, gossip or omission of the truth • Unable to express yourself • Impatient when listening to others • Incapable of speaking in the face of injustice • Suppressed

This chakra helps you *heal* **by...**	• Exploring how you were spoken to as a child. • Noticing patterns in conversations (when you speak up, when you listen and why). • Being curious around your inner voice, when you can speak the truth to yourself and others. • Processing moments that involved any verbal abuse, harsh criticism, or situations where you were lied to.
This chakra helps you *lead* **by...**	• Learning to communicate clearly and effectively. • Expressing yourself with truth, compassion and wisdom. • Practicing deep "level three" listening. Listen for what is said, not said, body language, and tone with full presence. • Advocating for yourself and others.
Shadow to explore	Lies
Affirmations	• I speak. • I listen. • My voice matters. • I have something to say. • My words can heal. • My truth has power. • I am honest. • I respond.
Ways of being	Integrity, responsive, patient, truthful, clear

Soften your jaw. Do you clench yours sometimes without realizing it? Most of us do. It's a stress response. It might feel like a physical way to hold things in. Ideas, frustrations, words we don't want to let spill out. On your next breath, really open the jaw on the exhale and maybe even flutter your lips. Notice how that invites some of that tension to be let go.

The work and themes of the lower chakras all come up here - to the throat - and can get stuck.

I know my purpose....but I can't articulate it.

I know I need boundaries to access creativity....but I don't know how to name them to this other person.

I feel my self-confidence growing in my leadership...but how do I speak to myself with love when doubts arise.

My heart aches for this person I love...but I don't know the words to use to tell them how I feel.

Notice your body as you read the information related to this chakra and leadership theme. Did you receive any insights from your body? Is there anything you want to say as a result of reading that information? Write or speak out loud in response to the idea that your words matter, and you have something to say in this lifetime.

Here's my invitation to take a minute and jot some notes down before jumping back in.

My Reflections :

Sound Element

The element associated with Leading with Truth, and the throat chakra, is SOUND. It's resonant and harmonious. It includes silence.

As we move up the energetic centers of the body, you'll notice the elements become less and less tangible. From the earth we can literally pick up with our hands, to the water we immerse ourselves in, to the fire that warms us from a distance and then the air we breathe but usually cannot see.

What sounds surround you - right here and right now? Tune into any loud or subtle sounds in your current environment and notice if these sounds are pleasant, unpleasant or neutral.

Sound can have a tremendous impact on our nervous system, and therefore, how we experience life.

Call to mind some sounds that you consider to be beautiful, harmonious, or powerful in a positive way. How do these sounds make you feel? What's the impact on your energy level, mood and emotions?

I'm always in awe of the power of familiar sounds. A favorite song, the predictable rhythm of waves, a friend's voice after a long time apart, how laughter almost always is contagious, relaxing into nature or city sounds that "feel like home". It's known that babies can hear their parent's voices while in the womb, and it's true. The Baby School, a research and education institution at Yale University for new and expectant parents found that, "Since the maternal voice is audible in utero, an infant starts to recognize their mother's voice from the third trimester."[14] I know without a doubt that the moment Gabby was born, she already knew us.

Get curious around what sounds, rhythms, harmonies feel like truth to you. What sounds connect you to your purpose, creativity and confidence. What sounds help you feel love more deeply? What music, poetry, conversations help you feel seen, heard and known?

In her incredible deep dive of the chakras, *The Wheels of Life*, Anodea Judith, PhD writes, "chakra 5 is the center related to communication through sound, vibration, self-expression, and creativity." and explains that "each chakra has its own associated seed sound which is said to contain the essence, and therefore the secrets, of that chakra."[15] Starting with the root chakra at the base and progressing upward to the crown chakra, the seed sounds are:

The Seed Sounds:

CROWN : (SILENCE)

THIRD EYE . . OM

THROAT . . . . . HAM

HEART . . . . .YAM

SOLAR PLEXUS . . . RAM

SACRAL . . . . .VAM

ROOT . . . . LAM

Mantra, and chanting, are beautiful ways to connect to the vibrations of each energetic center, and specifically to your throat. You get to experience both creating the sound as well as receiving it, from the inside out.

On the flip side, sounds can grate. A cacophonic sound can make our teeth grind and our goosebumps rise. We have physical reactions to the sounds we hear, and can be quickly brought back to painful memories when familiar sounds are evoked.

I find the absence of sound to be the most interesting part of this particular exploration. What is your relationship to silence? Notice if it brings about a sense of relief or loneliness.

After a busy day of work, getting in a quiet car might invite the first truly deep breath of the day. But arriving home to an empty house after a loved one moves out, the silence might be deafening.

When learning to meditate, a question that arises might be, "What do I do with all this quiet?" This is where the exploration of the sound element turns inward. We are creating space to hear our own inner voice. We'll learn more about that in the next chapter, accessing our intuition.

In the way that lightning and thunder are two different experiences and words to explain the same event, it's similar for sound and light. And also, truth and intuition.

You might "hear a voice of truth" sometimes, and "see the vision or the path forward", at others. Same same.

For now we'll focus on the sounds we create, we consume, and what we hear when we let ourselves be in silence.

 Sound

resonant
harmonious
silent
dissonant
rhythms
vibrations
reminds us to listen inward

Pause & Process

At this point, you've taken in a lot of information! I'm going to invite you to pause and process for a moment. Use the space below to note five takeaways or write some questions that may be swirling around for you related to the theme of truth.

An idea resonating with me is...

1

A question I have is...

2

I'm learning...

3

I'm wondering about...

4

A line of text that is sticking with me is...

5

Deepening Our Ability to Listen Matters

During my first year as an Assistant Principal of Instruction, I had the opportunity to be in a large leadership cohort that spanned throughout the year. We gathered with leaders across the country, and engaged in school visits as well as thoughtfully designed workshops. I was in full-on learning mode - notebooks open, hand raised, ready to share insights and ask questions.

I've always been this way with learning. My mind is quick, I love the validation of getting it "right", and I want the teacher to know I'm listening. (If you are rolling your eyes, I don't blame you, but it's the truth!)

What this younger version of me couldn't see was how much space I was taking up. In an effort to get the most out of *my* experience, I wasn't noticing how I was crowding out the experience for others.

During one session, I was seated next to this older woman, who had the opposite energy. She was seated in a relaxed way, leaned back, as if she had all the time in the world. After one of my eager shares, she asked if she could give me a piece of advice.

This was so many years ago, yet I remember it clear as day.

She looked at me with this wry smile and said, "Girl, if you want to be a leader, you have to calm down and LISTEN. You don't always have to be the first to speak."

I blushed hard. I felt deeply embarrassed.

But quickly, I decided to commit to one simple thing: *Listen first, then speak.* In a practical sense, that meant I could be the second person to speak if I wanted...but I would practice patience, open up the floor and see who else would come forward.

It's not an understatement to say that her comment made me a more impactful leader immediately.

Today, I pride myself on my ability to listen. I love learning about the levels of listening. I experiment with how long I can wait, and the impact that has on my clients, when I let them speak uninterrupted. It shifted how I approached my role as a leader in my school. I decided to lead more as a facilitator than a "sage on the stage". I made it my mission to build up as many teacher leaders as possible and be a supportive leader that made room for as many voices as possible.

I don't remember her name, but I am forever grateful that she was confident enough to speak some loving truth to me that day, *and* that I was able to listen.

Applications to Your Healing

THE THROAT CHAKRA HELPS YOU HEAL BY...

- Using your voice to release tension and let energy flow through you unrestricted through humming, song, speech, writing or your breath.

- Noticing patterns in conversations (when do you speak up, when do you listen and why).

- Being curious around your inner voice, when you can speak the truth to yourself and others.

- Processing moments that involved any verbal abuse, harsh criticism, or situations where you were lied to, either in childhood or adulthood.

Take some time to jot down any thoughts, reactions, sensations or emotions that are present in your experience **related to your healing.** Notice anything that is coming up now that you might want to revisit later before we dive into exploring the shadow of this energetic center.

My Reflections :

Exploring the Shadow: Lies

In my late twenties and early thirties, I dated a bit, as single people in big cities do. I like to say that I dated 10 versions of the same exact guy. Different names, different jobs - ultimately, the same experience. I felt unsettled in each one. Not quite chosen. There was adventure and sweet moments and fun times, but always an underlying anxiety. A sense that in an instant, it'd be over.

I did a fair amount of blaming externally as these relationships ended. With the gift of hindsight, I was able to see that I ultimately wasn't telling *myself* the truth. I didn't ever see them as "my person". How could I possibly? I wasn't fully being me. It was a classic example of saying things are "fine", when they're not.

I don't judge this younger version of myself - or them - anymore. I did the best I could with the tools I had. I was afraid of ending up single. I had no idea what a boundary was, let alone how to communicate one. My self-love and self-confidence game was seriously lacking and very much in progress. Of course I wasn't sure how to communicate internally or externally about what I deserved, what I wanted and how to end things when it was clear that this wasn't it.

Are there moments where you too have said things are "fine", when they weren't?

This feels like a "shadow light" version of lies, but to me it feels deeply important. Telling ourselves we're fine when we are not, is not the truth. Not the full truth that we know when we feel it.

That's the type of truth I want now. The type that reverberates from my very center. That roots my feet deeper, that evokes a warmth and sensation from my heart and down my arms. That fills my belly with confidence that I am worth a life that rings true, and so does everyone around me. A truth that emanates upwards and outwards and helps me remember the things that truly matter.

My marriage, like all relationships, isn't perfect. But it *feels* like truth. We try to speak to each other from the most honest of places. When I zoom out and look at the hum of our life together, it resonates with our authentic, most true selves, and that makes me happy. We get caught up in the drama of life, hectic schedules, self-made pressures and demanding deadlines, and our words can get clipped, our tones lacking harmony, just like anyone. Then we create some space, talk it out, and come back to a vibration of love and partnership.

It's something younger me would be really proud of.

What feels TRUE to you in your life?

If I were to sit down with you, right here and right now, and you trusted that I wanted to know the entire truth about how you are, what would you say?

What abundance might be possible if you allowed yourself to ask and answer big questions about how satisfied you are with your life, your relationships, your free time, your service in the world, your impact on your community, your sleep, your health? What could you let go of if you gave yourself permission to say the truth out loud?

It is not always eloquent. In fact, it's often messy until we've had more practice. I've learned to worry about that less. To stumble through my words until the truth finds its way out. Even if it sounds like this, "No...everything isn't ok. I don't know how I feel, but I don't feel good. I think it's because ..."

And I always feel the difference in my body. When I say I'm fine but I'm not, it's like there's this trapped energy circling, dancing, or throwing a tantrum inside my body.

Eventually, it'll find its way out.

Usually in a moment where I didn't want it to. One where I've reached a boiling point, and everything spills out at once, "I'm not only mad about this thing, but I'm also mad about the thing from last Tuesday. Oh, and last Sunday, too."

When we speak the truth, instead of lies, and release our attachment to what it means to have this truth spoken, the result is usually a feeling of lightness.

I'm ready for a new career.

This is what I need in my life.

This feels in alignment with who I am now.

I love you.

I deserve a raise.

My feelings were hurt.

I need help.

So, what's coming up for you in this shadow?

Are there lies big or small that you've been telling yourself or telling others?

What truth is asking to be released into the world?

"When we speak the truth instead of lies, the result is usually a feeling of lightness."

Exploring this chakra is an opportunity to get curious around your relationship to **truth, sound, and silence.** Are you able to find resonance and harmony in your day to day communication? What conditions support your ability to hear your inner voice and speak your truth into the world?

My Reflections :

All of this information influences how you communicate as a leader.

Applications to Your Leadership

> ### THE THROAT CHAKRA HELPS YOU LEAD BY...
>
> - Learning to communicate clearly and effectively, whether it's in person, through email, or any other form of spoken or written language.
>
> - Expressing yourself with truth, compassion and wisdom, especially in moments of significance.
>
> - Practicing deep listening where you listen for what is said, not said, body language, and tone with full presence. Rather than waiting to speak, give your full attention to being the listener.
>
> - Advocating for yourself and others, particularly those whose voices are underrepresented.

On the next page, take some time to jot down any thoughts, reactions, sensations or emotions that are present in your experience **related to your leadership.** Note any ideas, connections or musings you want to remember before we think about specific moments where you and I both have chosen to Lead with Truth.

My Reflections :

A Moment I Decided to Lead with Truth

When I decided to leave my role as Assistant Principal of Instruction, at a school where I'd spent almost a decade, it was heartbreaking. I loved the work, I loved the school, the teachers, the students and families. I deeply believed in the mission.

And yet, I couldn't deny the voice that told me it was time to go, at least for now. I deliberated for months, craving quiet walks in nature, processing with my husband, pouring my thoughts into my journal. Trying to quiet the outside noise in an effort to clearly hear that inner truth.

I made the final decision in the days I spent healing from my second pregnancy loss. It was on my favorite hike, crystal clear. It was time to go. Not only that, I decided that when I told people, I would tell them the truth.

The truth was, I needed time to heal from these two miscarriages. The truth was, my heart was broken. The truth was, I didn't know what was next. The truth was, I loved this school, and would do everything I could to ensure a smooth transition. The truth was, I loved them and the work, and it saddened me to go. The truth was, I knew it was the right thing to do at this time.

There's so much power in just stating things as they are.

I could've come up with countless other "cleaner" versions of this story. Maybe more "professional", but to me, it felt most honest to bring my full self to this decision, as I had brought my full self to the rest of my work.

It was the right move. I was met with so much humanity. So many hugs, shared tears, well wishes. So much compassion and gratitude.

I didn't know it then, but it set the path for the work I do now. That commitment to sharing honestly and bravely was a permission slip to lead from my full humanity. To merge wellness with leadership. To be able to share my heart, heal it and then lead from it in service to others.

I see the impact of that now. In conversations with clients where they meet the moment bravely, take a deep breath, and speak the truth. It's powerful. It's freeing. It's often preceded and followed by silence.

In that silence, that sacred space, we reconnect with our truest version of ourselves.

Whenever I feel like life is getting away from me, spinning too quickly, I reach for silence. That's where I can hear my inner truth the loudest. And once I hear it, it becomes undeniable. The rest, the sharing of this deep truth, naturally follows.

One of Your Stories

- Consider what you want to say about your voice and how it impacts the stories you tell as a leader in your life now.

- Write a story about truth. How does speaking, hearing, and living in alignment with truth show up in your life? What does it feel like?

- Think of a time either when you felt really balanced in this fifth chakra or this aspect of yourself. A time when you felt able to share your voice, listen to others and feel in resonance with your life.

- Think of a moment that brought healing to your inner and outer dialogues. It might be a moment where you apologized, broke the cycle of miscommunication or lies, rewrote inner narratives, or just finally said what you were aching to say.

My Reflections :

IT'S ALL CONNECTED

Embodiment Practices

The meditation and yoga can be practiced separately, or in either order. Experiment and see what feels most supportive in accessing your voice.

Meditation Script:

(tap into truth and clarity)

Find a comfortable seated or reclined position. Get as relaxed as you can, and take a few cleansing breaths. For this meditation, we'll experience some deep silence. I'll hold the space for us, and your job is just to be with yourself, and notice what you hear.

Begin with noticing the sounds outside of yourself.

- - - *(long held silence > 2min)* - - -

Now shift your attention to listening to your breath - see if you can differentiate between the outer sound of the breath and the inner sound of the breath.

- - - *(long held silence > 2 min)* - - -

Finally, take time to listen inward. What do you hear when you let all other sounds and distractions fall away?

- - - *(long held silence > 2min)* - - -

Begin to deepen your breath. Invite small movements into fingers and toes, circle ankles and wrists. Reach arms and legs in opposite directions and take a big stretch, maybe a sigh. Find your way up to a seat, grab your journal and write down any reflections from your practice.

My Reflections :

How to Practice

In this honest flow, let yourself be in a conversation with your body to help embody the sound element. Feel your throat and neck. Stay aware through your jaw. Notice what sounds and exhales want to come forth as you move.

Leading with Truth is all about communication, so consider how you are speaking and listening to your body as you find each posture. Allow this particular sequence to be harmonious.

Warm up

1 MOUNTAIN

2 FORWARD FOLD

3 HALFWAY LIFT

4 PLANK

5 COBRA

6 CAMEL OR KNEELING ANJALI MUDRA

-or-

7 PLANK

8 DOWNWARD FACING DOG

REPEAT 3X

Flows

1A HIGH LUNGE WITH HANDS INTERLACED

1B WARRIOR 3 WITH HANDS INTERLACED

1C FORWARD FOLD

1D RAGDOLL

RESET. REPEAT.

2A PUPPY   2B PLANK   2C CAMEL   2D HERO   R E S E T .   R E P E A T .

3A FOREARM PLANK   3B SPHINX   3C CHILD'S POSE   3D HERO   R E S E T .   R E P E A T .

4A EASY SEAT CAT   4B EASY SEAT COW   4C STAFF   4D REVERSE PLANK   R E S E T .   R E P E A T .

Cool Down

-or-

-or-

1 SHOULDER STAND OR HAPPY BABY   2 PLOW OR SEATED FORWARD FOLD   3 FISH   4 REST

how to engage with the theme of

TRUTH

body	**mind**

body

- Use your voice. Sing, speak, recite poetry, ask questions, tell a story.
- Practice chanting or humming.
- Tune into your body's signals when listening to others.
- Notice your jaw throughout the day, and actively relax it.
- Go out in nature and listen to all the sounds you hear.

mind

- Read! Anything that interests you. Notice how the words impact how you feel.
- Write! Anything that interests you. Freewrite, explore emotions, a story, a poem, etc.
- Speak to yourself with truth and love.
- Balance speaking and listening in a conversation.
- Meditate and listen inward.

soul

- Place your hands on a tree and listen.
- Experiment with silence and its impact on how you feel.
- Enjoy a sound bath.
- Meditate and free write journal afterward.
- Listen to music that evokes emotion - let whatever sounds emerge that want to.

work

- Practice present, active listening with colleagues.
- State your opinion simply, without qualifiers.
- Set community agreements that encourage equitable sharing norms.
- Create a gossip free culture.
- Advocate for underrepresented voices to join the conversation.

Leading
with
TRUTH
means...

- Practicing honesty and introspection.
- Listening for the deepest version of truth, in yourself and others.
- Embodying the sound element to tune into what resonates for you.
- Appreciating silence as well as sound.
- Trusting that you have a story that others deserve to hear.
- Exploring all the ways you can use your voice in the world - speaking your truth as well as listening to others.

PROMPTS FOR FURTHER REFLECTION

1. Listen to yourself speak this week - when do you hear yourself speaking truth really clearly? What else do you notice about this?

2. Notice the dynamics of communication this week. When do you show up as a listener? As the speaker? When does this feel in or out of balance?

3. Where do you hear your own inner voice most clearly? What are the conditions that allow this voice to speak loudly?

4. Consider how moving your body or sitting in stillness has impacted your connection to your leadership this week.

My Reflections : _____

_____
_____
_____
_____
_____
_____
_____
_____
_____
_____
_____
_____
_____
_____
_____

IT'S ALL CONNECTED

T R U T H

In Summary...

- Leading with Truth correlates to the throat chakra.

- Exploring, embodying and spending time tuning into the sound element can deepen your connection to this theme.

- Learning about, healing and loving your relationship to speaking out, using your voice, and sharing your truth with the world is important work. Consider all the ways your truth can advocate for more peace within yourself and in the world.

- Exploring your voice, the stories you tell yourself and how you lovingly speak to yourself is deeply connected to the prior themes. Get curious about connections here.

6 Lead with Intuition: "I See"

> "Intuition is really a sudden immersion of the soul into the universal current of life."
>
> – Paulo Coelho

Seeing with Clarity

Intuition can be a hard thing to explain. Here in the chapter about the third eye center, we explore what it means to see our visions clearly - both externally and internally.

You might be super familiar with moments in your life where you have connected to your intuition. Or this may feel brand new. We also connect to our intuition in our "gut", which for some is accessing the creative center of the sacral chakra, and others, the confident deep self-trust of the solar plexus chakra.

Either way, as we continue to move into the upper, more ethereal realms of these leadership themes and energetic centers, we must let go of the need to grasp onto the concrete with our hands, and instead, close our eyes, and lean into the unknown.

What does that feel like for you? Exciting? Terrifying?

Does it feel like surrender? Or anxiety?

There is no right or wrong answer here. Just notice your reaction.

It takes courage to be a visionary leader, and we'll explore that through the element of light. We'll notice how light and shadow work together, and how light supports our ability to see clearly.

In fact, there is much that inhibits our ability to see things as they truly are. We call this "illusion" and this is the shadow of the sixth chakra. Some of what clouds our vision are our expectations, our likes and dislikes, and desires for how we want things to be. Exploring this shadow can help illuminate the veils we unconsciously place on life, and hopefully see things more as they actually are. With clarity.

I can't wait to dive into this and support you connecting with your intuition in a deeper way.

What Does it Mean to Lead with Intuition?

To Lead with Intuition is all about trusting our ability to vision, imagine and see beyond the literal and tangible in the world. It's balancing the seen and the unseen. The hard facts and the warm sensation deep within.

Our culture loves to lift up the value of the concrete, the written, the documented and logical explanations. And there is so much value in this! Being able to collect data - from student assessment scores or the impact of nightly routines on how we sleep - there's so much to learn from crunching the numbers. Hear me when I say, data is powerful, and Leading with Intuition is not about discounting the information we can see, touch and feel.

Instead, accessing our ability to Lead with Intuition is about expanding our view to include that which we cannot see with our eyes. To look far and wide enough to learn from nature and its wisdom as well as deep enough inside our own beings to include the feeling, the gut instinct, the sensations that our body tunes us into.

Sounds very connected to our ability to Lead with Creativity, right? The flowing, water-like, more feminine energy of the sacral chakra is very connected to our ability to trust our intuition. To tap into the power of imagination, creative thinking, and balance. In the same way that knowing our purpose clearly supports our ability to Lead with Creativity, when we allow ourselves to trust in things we see AND do not see, we can experience more balance and greater evolution.

So what might this look like in the day to day?

I think a lot about the decisions leaders need to make. Decisions about where you send your kid to school. Decisions about what foods to feed yourself or your family. Decisions about what priorities matter to you in the season you are in. Decisions about what self care you might need after a long day of work. Decisions about how you spend your time, energy and attention moment to moment to moment.

On the next page, you'll have the opportunity to consider more deeply how you currently make decisions, and perhaps allow a little more room for intuition.

Mini exercise #1:
Decision Making Processes

- Make a list of all the decisions you've had to make, just today (or this week).

My Reflections :

- Now go back through and write a note about HOW you made each decision.
- Reflect on what you noticed: Which decisions did you look inward to answer? Which ones did you outsource? Which ones were easy because you make it every single day? Which ones were challenging because they were unique and new?

My Reflections : _____

_____

_____

_____

_____

_____

_____

_____

_____

_____

_____

_____

_____

When we overly depend on outward sources, and skip checking in with our intuition, we give our power away. Remember back to confidence? You have so much experience already. You have data within yourself. You have the ability to learn from history and nature and tune in to the expanse of time, and learn from yourself at any given moment.

I'm really quite practical, so I imagine you asking...*ok, so how do I do that?*

By allowing time and space.

Trusting yourself often happens best when you have time and space to block out other inputs. When we are in a constant stream of inputs - podcasts, others' opinions, social media, news, books, children's voices, etc - it can be hard to differentiate our thoughts from others, hear our own voice, or see our own vision.

Gifting yourself some time to look inward, especially when you need to make big choices, can support your ability to tap into and sense some new possibilities and imaginative solutions.

Mini exercise #2:
Your Wisest Self

- Consider a situation that you're facing right now related to your vision of yourself and your leadership. Let it be a big one - related to your purpose, what you want to create, or how you want to shine.
- Find a meditative position, sitting or standing or even laying down. Let your hands land on your body somewhere - maybe the belly, the heart, or connect with your third eye. Take a few breaths, slowing in and out through the nose.
- Then pick up a pen, and write, "Dear Wisest Self," and ask your question.
- When you feel ready, pick up a different color pen, and respond, from your Wisest Self.
- Let a dialogue unfold. Listen and watch for what answers arise.

My Reflections

How did your intuition, your Wisest Self, show up? Sounds? Images? Words? Feelings? Reflect on the process when you are complete.

My Reflections :

_____

_____

_____

_____

_____

_____

_____

_____

_____

_____

Repeat this exercise as often as you like to strengthen your connection with your intuition.

You have been accessing your intuition throughout this book already. As you continue to construct your vision for yourself as a leader, return to your notes and connect with that inner wisdom that is always available.

For now, let's learn more about this energetic center, the third eye chakra.

Name	Third eye chakra (ajna chakra)
Location in the body	Third eye, the space in between the eyebrows
Parts of the body related to this chakra	Face, eyes, ears, and central nervous system, brain, pineal gland
Color	Indigo, purple
Stone to work with	Amethyst, sodalite
Element	Light
When this chakra is *balanced*, you feel...	• Imaginative • Connected to dreams and inner knowing • Insightful • Focused • Clear headed in decision making
When this chakra is *out of balance*, you feel...	• Uninspired or not grounded in reality • Distracted • Forgetful of dreams or memories • Anxious or prone to headaches, insomnia and trouble with eyesight • Suspicious

This chakra helps you *heal* by...	• Exploring your relationship to your imagination. • Noticing your dreams and keeping a dream journal to track any themes. • Strengthening your relationship with your intuition. • Processing any experiences where you were told your ideas were "crazy" or unbelievable.
This chakra helps you *lead* by...	• Articulating a clear vision for yourself as a leader. • Expanding the dream of the impact you want to make in the world. • Trusting in your decisions and your ability to bring visions into reality. • Seeing the big picture as well as the details.
Shadow to explore	Illusion
Affirmations	• I see. • I trust. • I dream. • I am intuitive. • I envision. • I have clarity. • I imagine. • I have access to inner wisdom.
Ways of being	Imaginative, visionary. contemplative. trusting, intuitive

What are you noticing about how this information lands with you compared to some of the earlier chapters? Is it lighter? Less emotional? Less dense? Did you experience any insights from the body? Or do you feel more activation in the mind? What questions are coming up for you? Create some quiet time to reflect on the idea that when you are aligned within, you can see yourself and others clearly. You have a vision for a better world and you know your place in it.

Invitation to take a minute and jot some notes down before jumping back in.

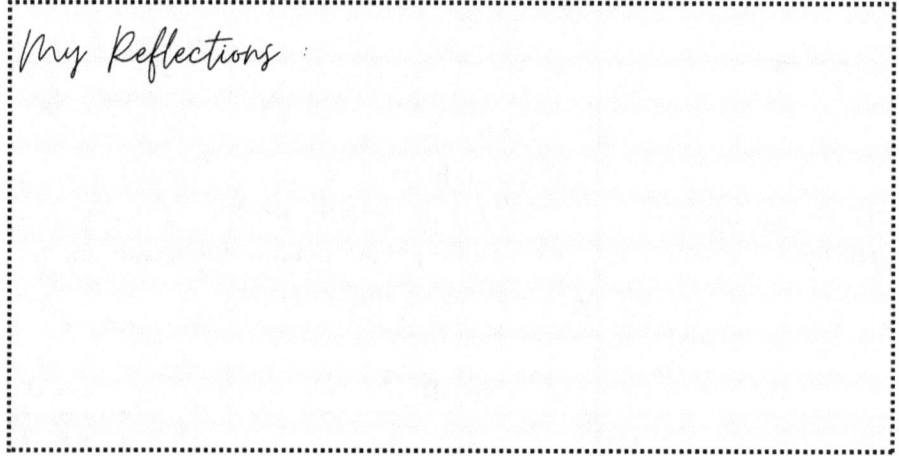

My Reflections :

Light Element

The element associated with Leading with Intuition, and the third eye chakra, is LIGHT. It's clear, it's illuminating, it brings things into focus.

We take in so much information through the eyes, all aided by light.

Take a moment and notice all the sources of light around you. Get curious about the types of light that help you see more clearly - in your home, and out in the world.

Are there types of light throughout the day that are more activating? More calming? Which do you prefer?

As you explore your home, or stores, or as you drive around - take inventory of how lights are positioned, placed, or where they are absent. Notice what they are highlighting and what they are hiding.

You might experiment with when and how you use or avoid certain types of light to wind down for bed and to ease into the day. Blue light, from screens or artificial light, has significant effects on circadian rhythms and sleep, which impacts our overall wellness.[16]

If you are lucky enough to be somewhere with minimal light pollution, notice the subtle light from the moon and stars at night. Feel how your eyes adjust, and how you have to move with care, intentionally finding your way in the darkness.

If you get the chance to witness a rainbow, take an extra moment to marvel at the separation of light that is revealed. Let your eyes travel through each color with patience.

All these invitations are a reminder that we cannot see everything at once. We have to turn our bodies, our eyes, our awareness and attention towards what it is we want to see. We must choose.

This agency could be related to the books we read, the movies we watch, the content we consume in any way - are we choosing to see a situation from a wide range of perspectives? Where do we give our attention? Where are we directing our eyes, and what are we intentionally avoiding?

Especially when we have the responsibility of making decisions that impact others - are we shedding light on the situation in a way that feels just, inclusive and equitable?

When we're making decisions for ourselves, we can look at our lives through a lens of strength, curiosity, beauty and abundance. We can actively choose to shine a metaphorical light on all parts of ourselves and see them as part of the whole.

The relationship between light and shadow is the last piece I want to explore here.

In each chapter, the chakra has a shadow to explore. It's hard work. It's messy, often emotional. It's easy to want to avoid what lives in the shadows - but the shadows exist. And they are in relationship to the light. If we can see ourselves in the same way... that the shadow helps us understand the light, that it is lovable as well, we can put the pieces of ourselves together, integrate and find wholeness. Then maybe we can marvel at how one moment of grief paves the way for more spaciousness and joy. How a "no" in one moment creates a "yes" in another.

How we explore the light and the shadow is through svadhyaya, self study. One of my teachers, Seane Corn, writes in her book *Revolution of the Soul*, that, "once we commit to the work, we must move full-on into svadhyaya, the yogic path of self-awareness and self-reflection...svadhyaya is the soul's work, the soul's investigation into how things are. It invites us to look at experience as experience - without labeling it."[17] It's about having clear vision, seeing things as they truly are.

When we can choose to let ourselves be seen first by *ourselves* - in our entirety - and then by others, we begin to see others in the full spectrum of their existence as well.

 Light

illuminating
clarifying
bright
focused
beautiful
imaginative
reminds us to take multiple perspectives

Pause & Process

At this point, you've taken in a lot of information! I'm going to invite you to pause and process for a moment. Use the space below to note five takeaways or write some questions that may be swirling around for you related to the theme of intuition.

An idea resonating with me is...

1

A question I have is...

2

I'm learning...

3

I'm wondering about...

4

A line of text that is sticking with me is...

5

Your Healing & Leadership: Application of "Leading with Intuition"

Trusting Our Inner Wisdom Matters

One of the most powerful meditations I've practiced is a study in alchemy. One of my favorite teachers, Susannah Freedman, sometimes offers this specific meditation at the end of class. Here's how it goes.

You sit up tall, close your eyes, and begin to breathe. Then you begin to breathe in through the heart, and out through the heart, imagining the breath entering and exiting this fourth chakra. As you know even more intimately now, it's the center of love, grief, compassion, and altruism.

After a few breaths, we shift to breathing in through the heart, and out through the third eye, the space in between the eyebrows.

Whenever I practice this, I immediately sit up straighter. I fill the body with breath, and truly imagine the breath entering and filling the heart, swirling around, then traveling up the spine to leave the body right in between the eyes. This seat of intuition and wisdom.

During one class, here I was, breathing in through the heart and out through the third eye, and with every single breath, I was able to see and feel a memory of grief.

The loss of my dad.

Heartache over lost friendships or relationships.

Miscarriage number 1.

Miscarriage number 2.

Leaving a job I loved.

And with each one, I saw the healing, and the pieces of wisdom that were born from those moments of grief.

My independence.

My depth and care for others.

My loyalty to those I love.

My commitment to healing my body.

My beautiful daughter and my choice to be so present with her.

My more spacious and intentional life.

The birth of my business and its service to others.

In that moment, I felt the creation of wisdom. The bank of internal knowledge that I now draw from easily - it's not random. It's connected. The grief, the heartache, the love, the life experiences we have - all of it is churned up, turned over, inside out, woven together to make us who we are now. It clarifies what we know now.

The connection between intuition and wisdom is so clear. Intuition being about our ability to see and know beyond reason, and wisdom being the application of our knowledge and lived experience. It's all within us *and* available when we look way outside ourselves. When we see loved ones grow and change throughout their lives. When we watch seasons change. If we pause and look up at the stars and remember how finite we are.

This is the perspective yoga helps me keep - that all of the events in our lives are not just "sad" or "happy", "good" or "bad". That within a moment we can experience great loss and grow as a result. We can be both grounded and imaginative. We can be logical and believe in magic.

Applications to Your Healing

THE THIRD EYE CHAKRA HELPS YOU HEAL BY...

- Exploring your relationship to your imagination and your dreams, maybe through keeping a dream journal to track any themes.

- Strengthening your relationship with your intuition by allowing space in your day, in your body, and in your life to look, listen, and feel inward.

- Processing any experiences where you were told your ideas were "crazy" or unbelievable.

- Transforming experiences into wisdom through intentional meditation or reflective practices.

Take some time to jot down any thoughts, reactions, sensations or emotions that are present in your experience **related to your healing.** Notice anything that is coming up now that you might want to revisit later before we dive into exploring the shadow of this energetic center.

My Reflections :

Exploring the Shadow: Illusion

You know those fun mirrors that are usually in Halloween houses or at county fairs? The ones that distort the image in silly ways, making you look way taller, or shorter or giving you 10 eyes? I can imagine my siblings and I looking in those mirrors, giggling at how ridiculous we look, knowing full well that our eyes are playing tricks on us. We are still here, in the same bodies, but what we see....looks totally different.

I haven't taken Gabby to see any of those yet, but she loves Halloween. It's the same idea. An opportunity to put on a costume and alter the way we are seen or the way we see others. The masks! The outfits! The acting that naturally comes along with it. She loves it. And receiving candy, of course.

It's mostly all fun, but there can be plenty of scariness that creeps into Halloween. I learned that I would not be able to sleep through the night after watching scary movies as a young adult, and now I understand more about why. Our minds and bodies can't really tell the difference between what's real and what's imagined. So even though I can logically know that I'm watching something scary, played by actors, I can still find myself holding my breath, clutching someone's hand next to me and feel my heart rate pick up.

That's what this shadow, illusion, reminds me of. Illusion is casting a view over our reality so that it distorts our vision, our view of reality, something either inside or outside of us that makes it impossible to see things as they really are.

On a potentially less scary note, social media comes to mind.

Even those most committed to showing up "authentically" on social media are only showing a fraction of the moments of their lives. These shared moments are then strung together in a way that can easily create a distorted reality.

The woman who is always perfectly pulled together.

The immaculate house.

The overly "brave" voice in the comments speaking in a way they never would face-to-face with someone.

These illusions come from within ourselves, depending on our previous life experiences. Our mind is constantly taking in information, making meaning, assigning stories, sending experiences into long term memory, and creating new beliefs. In yoga, we refer to these beliefs and patterned ways of thinking as samskaras, or grooves.

The beliefs - or stories - of how we view ourselves, others or the world, change the way we think, act and show up.

But the fact that these beliefs, stories, can be rewritten proves to us that they are just an illusion. If I choose to operate from a new belief "abundance is everywhere" rather than an old one "there isn't enough", I completely shift the way I'm able to show up in the world. I can then seek out the beauty, act from generosity, celebrate and share, knowing that it will be replenished and that none of it is "mine" to hold on to anyway.

When we shed old stories, we can see one another with more compassion. We can see our sameness rather than our perceived differences.

It's like if we stopped looking in those silly mirrors, and instead, turned to face one another. Looked directly at each other, face-to-face. It's so much easier to see clearly. The illusion fades, replaced with clarity that you and I are both humans on a similar path.

So how do we commit to seeing ourselves and each other clearly?

When I am too focused on the day-to-day minutiae of life, or caught up in the news cycle, it's easy to slip into the illusion of worst case scenarios. To believe the stories of lack, scarcity or despair.

Taking time to be embodied, feel grounded, connect with loved ones, witness the resilience of nature, look for the helpers, seek out hope and abundance on purpose can shift our perspective.

When we give ourselves more space, and intentionally look for the light, we can see the truth more clearly - that everything changes, nothing is permanent, and that love is at the center of most things, including us.

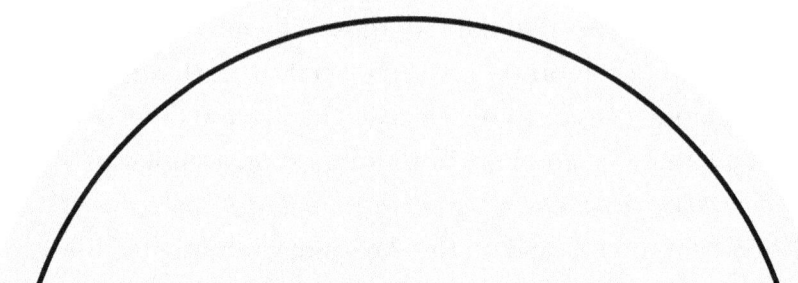

"The illusion fades, replaced with clarity that you and I are both humans on a similar path."

Exploring this chakra is an opportunity to get curious around your relationship to **intuitive messages, wisdom, and the way you see the world.** Are you able to see your soul clearly? What conditions support your ability to experience clarity, vision, and a perspective of wholeness?

My Reflections :

All of this information influences how you see yourself as a leader.

Applications to Your Leadership

THE THIRD EYE CHAKRA HELPS YOU LEAD BY...

- Articulating a clear vision for yourself as a leader - for the work you want to bring into the world, the team you want to lead, or for your family.

- Expanding the dream of the impact you want to make in the world - this includes using concrete information as well as knowing how to tune into your intuition and find the balance that works for you.

- Trusting in your decisions and your ability to bring visions into reality.

- Seeing the big picture as well as the details. Especially when leading a team, holding on to your ability to see the larger view supports everyone having clear direction and feeling grounded.

On the following page, take some time to jot down any thoughts, reactions, sensations or emotions that are present in your experience **related to your leadership**. Note any ideas, connections or musings you want to remember before we think about specific moments where you and I both have chosen to Lead with Intuition.

My Reflections :

A Moment I Decided to Lead with Intuition

There are countless moments where intuition has played a pivotal role in my leadership, but since I'm here, writing to you, the vision for this very book is the example I want to share with you right now.

Picture this. It was early November, 2023, and I was on a Mind, Body, Business Retreat in Baja, Mexico, walking along the beach at sunrise. I had shed the layers of busyness and hustle and finally settled into the flow of being on retreat - which is not something I do often. This was definitely the farthest from home I've gone in a while, and the power of that unplugging was magical.

As I was taking in the sounds of the water lapping, and the colors changing in the sky, I got the inspiration. The download. The vision.

I just knew I wanted to connect leadership identity and evolution with the healing power of the chakras. Leadership through the chakras. I immediately typed into my phone the themes, all 7. Boom. Done.

Now, what to do with it? In my vision, I saw people gathering in community - to practice yoga, discussing their leadership connections, healing and growing individually and collectively.

I didn't yet know how I wanted to offer this information, but the seed idea...I could feel it in my bones, in my soul. *I just knew.* I have done so much healing through working with these shadows, these themes, through practice. Of course I am uniquely meant to share it with you. That's what intuition feels like to me. It's like, "duh, of course this is the next step."

Simultaneously, I have always known I was meant to write a book in my life. Topic? Unsure. But the vision has always been there. Again, a deep knowing.

The ideas swirled and shapeshifted for a few months. I was trying to figure out how to create a community to facilitate this growth and healing and write a book, and what should the book even be about?

It seems silly now, because hindsight is 20/20, but I had this nagging feeling, like I was just missing something - like I left the water running or forgot to take my vitamins. You know that feeling?

Then, one weekend, Gabby, Jason and I were having a lazy, spacious Saturday afternoon, and in that space, the intuition came through with ultimate clarity.

The book I knew I was meant to write and the community workshops I was envisioning were meant to be *together*.

I grabbed my big poster paper, and it all flowed out. The workshops, the chapter titles, the mantras, the themes. In 20 minutes it was all down there and the clarity was like a veil lifted. I could see it. I knew people would say yes. I knew this was the story I was meant to tell.

And so here we are. This book in your hands. My heart is feeling so healed through this process of writing, remembering, sharing, and holding space with a community along for the ride.

A vision realized.

One of Your Stories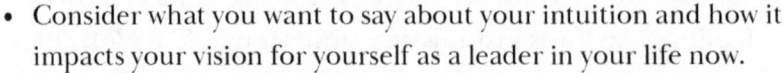

- Consider what you want to say about your intuition and how it impacts your vision for yourself as a leader in your life now.

- Write a story about trust. What helps you trust yourself? How does trust with yourself relate to your ability to trust others?

- Think of a time you felt balanced in this sixth chakra or this aspect of yourself. A time you were able to show up with clarity, vision and trust, for yourself or someone else.

- Think of a time you healed something related to your intuition. It might be a moment where you decided to look inward rather than outside of yourself for answers, or a moment where you began to trust the vision you have for your own life.

IT'S ALL CONNECTED

Embodiment Practices

The meditation and yoga can be practiced separately, or in either order. Experiment and see what feels most supportive in awakening your intuition.

Meditation Script
(tap into intuition and clarity)

Find a comfortable seated position, either seated or lying down. Take a few moments to arrange the body so that you are extra comfortable. Then turn your attention to your breath. Take a few full, deep breaths in through your nose, and exhale completely.

Imagine a wave of golden warm light was pouring through the crown of the head, and slowly seeping its way into every part of your body. Visualize this warm light filling up your spine, illuminating the face and neck. Feel this golden warmth expanding in the lungs, and down the arms, traveling through the belly and hips and wrapping the legs in its warmth. Imagine the entire body lit up, encased in this light and warmth.

Imagine that this light now takes the form of the most beautiful pair of sunglasses you have ever seen. When you put these sunglasses on, you can see your life through whatever "lens" you choose.

Begin by infusing these golden sunglasses with the lens of abundance. Take your time to place the glasses over your eyes, and see your life as so incredibly abundant. Notice what shimmers and catches your attention. What is already there is a reminder of your abundant life. Take a deep breath in...and out.

Imagine you now infuse the glasses with the ability to see through the lens of love. Place them back over your eyes and imagine you can look around. What do you see that shines with love? What stands out? What do you notice?

Take a deep breath. Choose one last lens. You pick this time... maybe it's success, confidence, trust, hope, connection. When you are ready, place the glasses over your eyes and see your life through this lens. What do you see? What's there that you can notice more clearly? How does it feel to look through this lens?

Take a cleansing breath. Remove the glasses and notice that they absorb back into you, always available when you need them. You can begin to call awareness back into the physical body, and begin to deepen your breath.

Grab your journal and note down anything from this visualization that gave you some insight.

My Reflections :

INTUITION
Yoga Sequence

How to Practice

Throughout this intuitive flow, use your inner eye to move between poses to help embody the light element. Play with closing your eyes as you flow, and trust your body's wisdom to guide you from shape to shape.

Leading with Intuition is all about trust, so consider how you are looking inward for guidance in each posture. Allow this particular sequence to be clarifying.

Warm up

1 MOUNTAIN ANJALI MUDRA

2 MOUNTAIN UPWARD SALUTE

3 FORWARD FOLD

4 HALFWAY LIFT

REPEAT 5X

5 PLANK

6 CHATURANGA

7 UPWARD FACING DOG

8 DOWNWARD FACING DOG

Flows

1A WARRIOR ONE

1B HUMBLE WARRIOR

1C WARRIOR ONE

1D PYRAMID

RESET. REPEAT.

2A CHILD'S POSE WITH PRAYER HANDS

2B DOWNWARD FACING DOG

2C CHAIR, REVOLVED TWIST

2D FORWARD FOLD

RESET. REPEAT.

3A MOUNTAIN

3B STANDING BIG TOE

3C STANDING BIG TOE - REVOLVED

3D FORWARD FOLD

RESET. REPEAT.

4A CHAIR

4B STANDING PIGEON

4C EAGLE

4D FORWARD FOLD

RESET. REPEAT.

Cool Down

1 SUPPORTED BRIDGE

2 LEGS UP WALL

3 SUPINE TWIST

4 REST

how to engage with the theme of

INTUITION

body

- Walk in nature and take notice.
- Feel your body's sensations in certain moments and reflect on what insight the body has.
- Practice yoga with eyes closed and trust your body.
- Schedule wide-open time to follow your intuition.
- Apply direct pressure on the third eye in child's pose.

mind

- Include daily rituals to strengthen the ability listen inward (i.e. meditation, mindfulness, time in nature).
- Free write in your journal to uncover old beliefs.
- Document your dreams.
- Imagine your life fully aligned with a mantra or affirmation.
- Do visualization work at the beginning of the day to live out your vision for your life.

soul

- Create a vision board or journal about your visions and dreams for yourself and the world.
- Use Tarot cards or Angel cards.
- Share your visions and your dreams with loved ones.
- Spend time with people who make you feel seen.
- Create a ritual to check in with your intuition when making decisions.

work

- Calendar time to be self reflective and introspective.
- Make decisions from both logical and intuitive spaces.
- Do vision work (I envision...) for yourself as a leader in your family, work or life.
- Choose your lens "curiosity, love, etc." from which to view life.
- Collaborate with colleagues to strengthen a collective vision.

Leading
with
INTUITION
means...

- Embodying the light element so you can trust in what you see as well as the wisdom that comes from within.
- Having a clear vision for yourself and your purpose in the world.
- Connecting to a sense-based way of making decisions.
- Creating the conditions where you can access your intuition on a regular basis.
- Tapping into your imagination, dreams and visionary energy.
- Knowing how to adjust your perspective, see the larger picture and learn wisdom from previous experiences.

PROMPTS FOR FURTHER REFLECTION

1. Notice what you see in your surroundings this week. Take in the beauty, the colors, the variety, the abundance. Describe anything you noticed that was new and surprising.

2. Identify when you have accessed intuition for yourself. Intuition is a sort of "trusting what we cannot see". What are some things that you trust in, that you cannot see with your eyes?

3. Describe a small moment this week where you trusted your intuition - no moment is too small.

4. Consider how moving your body or sitting in stillness impacted your connection to your leadership this week.

My Reflections : _____

_____

_____

_____

_____

_____

_____

_____

_____

_____

_____

_____

_____

_____

_____

_____

_____

_____

_____

IT'S ALL CONNECTED

IT'S ALL CONNECTED

INTUITION

In Summary...

- Leading with Intuition correlates to the third eye chakra.

- Exploring, embodying and spending time tuning into the light element can deepen your connection to this theme.

- Learning about, healing and loving your relationship to your intuition, believing in your visions and dreams, and unlearning harmful false beliefs helps you evolve as a leader. Consider all the ways your leadership can create positive change.

- Exploring your beliefs, trusting your unique wisdom and following your intuition can guide you on paths you never thought possible. Look inward for guidance here.

7 Lead with Connection: "I Know"

> "When you are balanced in this vital energy center, you are wise, you are open - minded, you have a sense of spiritual connection, and you can experience yourself, each other, the planet and God as unified."
>
> ~Seane Corn, *Revolution of the Soul*

Remembering with Wisdom

At this point, we have journeyed through so much together. Your purpose, your creativity, your confidence, your love, your ability to hear and speak the truth, your intuition. Here, at our final leadership theme Leading with Connection, what if I asked you to release your attachment to all of it?

This final chakra is at the crown of the head. It's the place where we remember that you are not alone, we are spiritual beings having a human experience, and that everything is connected and everything is temporary. It's where we may or may not feel as if we are a channel for this purpose. That's it's not actually you, but *through* you, in service to others.

Exploring the shadow side of the crown chakra may feel like a relief, because the shadow of this energetic center is attachment. This means that all the previous shadow work you've done? All the things you have unearthed?

You get to let them go.

The harder part about working with the shadow of attachment is contending with our egos and also holding our hands open wide to release our attachment to any of the "good" things that have come our way as well.

In the context of this book, I could say that "I" had all of these ideas, but in truth, I have felt them pour through me. Just as the idea for the book is, yes, born from the experiences in my life and what I've studied, the experience of writing it is that of being a vessel. Of listening and answering the call.

I wonder if you've had moments like that throughout these chapters. Moments where you couldn't really explain where the answers came from, but you know they are real just the same. My fingers typed these words, but a force bigger than me helped the vision and the ideas come to life. It's hard to explain concepts here at the crown chakra, this final leadership theme. The element is thought, or consciousness, and it's all around and within us.

In this chapter, I want to offer both simple, practical suggestions for how we can engage with this theme in everyday moments. I also want to ask big questions that we don't yet know the answers to. I want to expand our thinking, challenge our current schema, and invite us to dive deeper into the workings of the mind. To use its powers for good.

If this very ethereal leadership theme is harder to grasp, know that it's ok. The information you are meant to know right now will find you. The rest will revisit when the time is right.

What does it mean to Lead with Connection?

To Lead with Connection is to recognize and remember our shared humanity. To see all of us as humans on a journey, perfect and flawed at the same time, deserving of love and freedom, all worthy of existence.

Another way to explain Leading with Connection is to see the Divine in ourselves, in each other, in the planet, and be at peace with the temporary nature and connectedness of all things. To maintain this spiritual connection as we go about our daily lives.

What would shift in the way we treated each other, and spoke to ourselves, if we saw one another as part of the same divine spark?

Would we care less about the clothes we wear, and how much we weigh? Would we be kinder in traffic jams or discussing politics? Would we still keep the structures in place that aim to separate?

Leading with Connection can be a vast endeavor - like seeking spiritual enlightenment - or it can be as simple as creating a few moments at the beginning of a meeting to check in with people. To breathe and ask them genuinely, how are you? And wait for the real answer.

When I think about how I want to Lead with Connection, I inevitably think about my daughter. Which makes me smile, because I thought I would write something about leadership coaching. But no, of course it's her. *It's always her.*

I want to Lead with Connection as her mother. I desperately want to be able to remember our shared humanity in moments where she is - or I am - having huge feelings. I want to erase any moment I lost my cool or felt annoyed or overwhelmed and my ego got in the way of my KNOWING that she is a divine spark - a perfect soul on a journey. Just like you. And just like me. I want to keep that knowing as I let my own shame and guilt for not being a perfect mother creep into my self-talk. I want to remember that I too am an expression of the divine, on this human journey doing the best I can to learn and grow and heal. When I do remember that, everything softens.

I release judgment. I release shame. I release guilt. I choose love. I choose presence and connection and being together.

I remember that she is learning, and I am learning, and together we are learning.

As Ram Dass says, we're all walking each other home.

Mini exercise #1:
Pathways to Connection

Consider someone you love. Maybe it's a family member, a partner or dear friend.

Can you identify a moment where you felt separate from them? Write about it.

What helped you remember that you two are connected? What helped you heal?

Questions that might prompt even deeper reflection:
- What do you believe?
- What do you believe in?
- What helps you trust?

My Reflections :

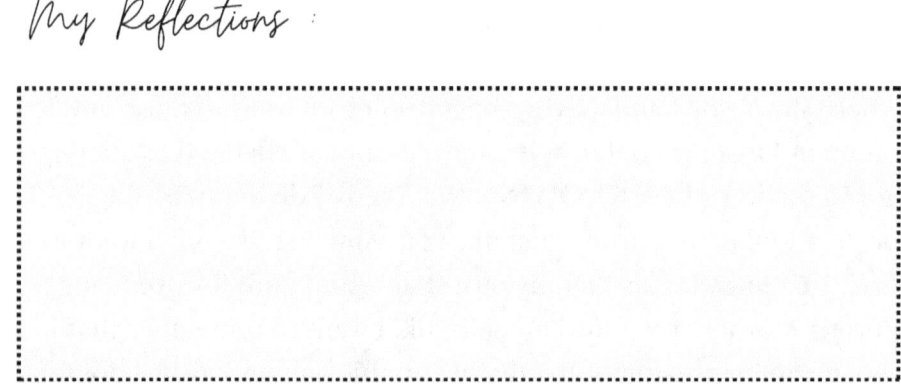

This is the invitation in this theme: to identify what it is that helps you remember. To know and use what gives you the perspective, the wisdom, the understanding, the remembrance to come back to love, and ultimately, to connection.

For me - space, time, breath, nature, song, writing, grounding touch, movement all bring me back to the present moment. To my body. They get me out of the spin of the mind and when the dust settles, it feels like an exhale.

Oh, right. You and me? We're connected.

What makes my heart ache, and what leads many of us to dissociate or choose numbness or scroll past horrific images, is when we allow ourselves to witness the separation that exists all around us. It's everywhere. It's in our systems, our policies, our borders, our ideologies, and it seeps into our bones, into our beliefs. It sends messages of, "this is mine and this is yours. I am here and you are there."

Yoga, by definition, means "union" or "to yoke". Another way to say this is to "put together" or "re-member".

When we practice yoga, we know the work is to choose connection. To intentionally put things together as often as we can. To sit in discomfort, to ask hard questions, to see one another in our humanity and remember that we are not separate. As Maya Angelou said, "The truth is, no one of us can be free until everybody is free."

Life is lived one moment at a time - so why not aspire to fill them with more compassion, more truth and more love?

Be on the lookout for moments of wisdom, moments where you connect the current moment to something larger. Feel when your body, mind and heart whisper, "Oh! We've been here before". We can call upon these past experiences, and apply the learnings to the current context.

Mini exercise #2:
Gaining Spacious Perspective

Imagine a current problematic or stressful situation in your life. Get into the details in your mind.

Notice what's happening in your body.

Now, imagine you could zoom way out in this scenario. See yourself from a distance, and then keep going, zooming farther and farther still. Look down on this situation from this spacious, way up high, perspective.

What becomes clear for you here?

Again, notice your body. How does your body feel with this broader perspective?

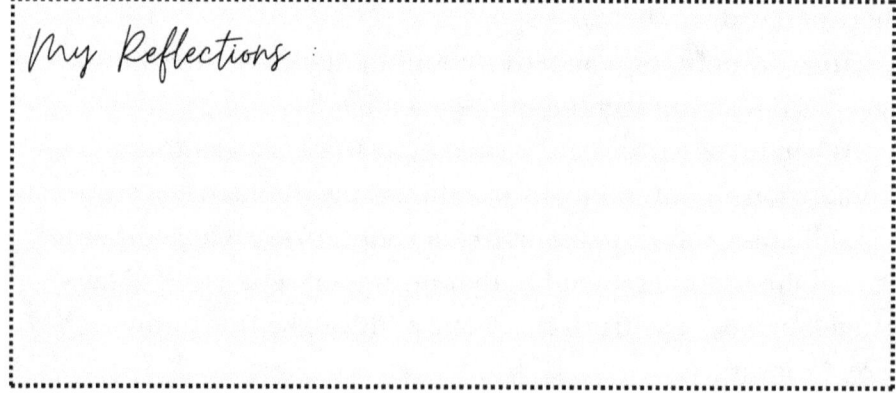

My Reflections :

This is the wisdom of love. It reminds us that this moment is connected to the one that came before and the one after, and that we are all connected to each other. *My humanity is connected to your humanity. So this issue here, it's nothing we can't figure out.*

Now, let's dive into some information about the crown chakra, the sahasrara chakra, the energetic center of the body associated with connection and wisdom.

Name	**Crown chakra (sahasrara chakra)**
Location in the body	Top of the head, space above the head
Parts of the body related to this chakra	All the systems of the body, including the skin (dermal), hormonal and the nervous system, pituitary and hypothalamus glands
Color	White, violet
Stone to work with	Clear quartz, selenite
Element	Thought (or consciousness)
When this chakra is *balanced*, you feel...	• Wise • Spiritually connected to (God, nature, spirit, higher power, the Divine, etc) • Peaceful • Transcendent • Open-minded
When this chakra is *out of balance*, you feel...	• Judgmental • Disenchanted • Materialistic • Obsessive in thoughts • Forgetful

This chakra helps you *heal* **by...**	• Processing your relationship to religion, spirituality and faith. • Practicing mindfulness and meditation to calm the fluctuations of the mind. • Releasing whatever you are gripping, learning to practice nonattachment. • Seeing everything and everyone as connected.
This chakra helps you *lead* **by...**	• Conceptualizing the larger picture as you move through daily work. • Remembering the individual as well as the collective in decisions and experiences. • Observing thought loops, and using introspection to guide your leadership. • Bringing a "human first approach" to your work.
Shadow to explore	Attachment
Affirmations	• I remember. • I know. • I am a vessel for love and light. • I am connected. • I am divine light. • I am at peace. • I am reflective. • We are all connected.
Ways of being	Wise, content, introspective, spiritual, peaceful

What are you noticing as you read through that information? How is your mind working through it? What do you feel in your body?

We are here at the most esoteric of all the chakras. It's harder to grasp and put our hands around the way we could with the solid earth of the root chakra. Take a deep breath, find some grounding. Jot down any thoughts and questions, and then proceed as you feel ready.

My Reflections :

Thought Element

The element associated with Leading with Connection, and the crown chakra, is THOUGHT, or consciousness. It's limitless, connected to all things, it is where and how we remember.

When we become aware of the running commentary that occurs in our mind, we realize that "thought" is absolutely an element that we can work with. In *The Untethered Soul*, Singer writes, "creating thoughts, holding onto thoughts, recalling thoughts....all require a tremendous amount of energy."[18]

Our thoughts have the ability to ground us to the here and now, or send us on spirals of anxiety and worry. The relationship between this first theme - purpose, grounding, belonging - and the last are essential. We have to be rooted enough to the present moment to allow the spaciousness of the mind to open. The wisdom of nature reminds us how connected we are to each other and all of humanity, while it doubles as the concrete way to ground the body and open the mind to expansive possibilities.

Exploring the conscious mind is really quite simple. We pay attention.

It can look like sitting in meditation, or giving yourself time in between your daily activities to feel your feet on the earth, and set your intention. It's tuning into the thoughts you're experiencing and the impact they have on your day-to-day life.

It's about bringing conscious awareness to everything we do - the words we speak, where we buy our food, who we vote for, how we care for our earth - and our thoughts as well. It's befriending the mind and recognizing that the ego is not who we are.

When we actually do all this... It's a lot. So we get glimpses. Moments of insight.

It often happens by making smaller connections in our own life, perhaps while journaling on the couch, brief pauses where we see that we are not static beings. That we learn and grow and evolve. That because of our experiences and choices and intentional living, we can impact the way we experience life. That we are capable of rewriting mindsets, starting new habits, new discoveries, self love, forgiveness.

One of my favorite leaders to learn from is Elena Aguilar. In her book *Onward*, she writes about telling empowering stories by "being aware of thoughts, recognizing and shifting distorted thoughts, uprooting the problematic core beliefs that lie below unproductive thoughts, crafting new stories, recognizing organizational stories around us, and sharing your stories."[19]

As we work with the element of thought, we intentionally witness our own evolution.

Reflective practices like meditation, coaching, and journaling create the space - often by reducing rumination[20] - to observe ourselves integrating wisdom, and pause long enough to say, *wow - that shifted in me.* I'm different now because I went through this season in my life. *This is who I am now, given all that I have learned and experienced.*

Working with the thought element is taking the wise seat of the witness - observing the moment while we're in it. It's nuanced, but it's the difference between over-identifying with an emotion, and being able to notice that you are experiencing an emotion. It's being able to say "I am in a moment of stress." vs "I am stressed". When we recognize an emotion passing through, we can remember - *I've been here before. I have tools for this. It won't last forever.*

Put simply, it's noting and creating space in between the thoughts. In that space, we can glimpse the bigger picture. We remember.

Thought

limitless
connected
wise
aware
ethereal
conscious
reminds us to see the big picture

Pause & Process

At this point, you've taken in a lot of information! I'm going to invite you to pause and process for a moment. Use the space below to note five takeaways or write some questions that may be swirling around for you related to the theme of connection.

An idea resonating with me is...

1

A question I have is...

2

I'm learning...

3

I'm wondering about...

4

A line of text that is sticking with me is...

5

Remembering That We Are Connected Matters

Giving birth to my daughter was the single most powerful, connective experience I have ever had, and I was forever changed as a result.

I promise to not be graphic. What I really want to share with you is about my heart.

At this point, you know about my two losses leading up to my pregnancy with Gabrielle. You know the grief I felt, and how it is connected to fear, guilt and shame. Despite feeling mostly wonderful throughout my pregnancy, I struggled to relax until she was born. There was always this little voice in the back of my head telling me not to get my hopes up.

Not helpful, right? This is why I spent so much time on long walks, on my yoga mat, journaling, learning, and healing. Trying to stay embodied.

In the hours leading up to her birth, I was in deep relationship with my body. I wanted to safely proceed without intervention if possible - I wanted to be present for each moment. Feel the changes, be with the sensations and work with my baby until she or he arrived.

Our incredible doula reminded me to stay connected to my breath and my body when she could hear in my voice that my mind was taking me elsewhere. With her hands literally over my heart, she'd say "stay here". It was the most intense, beautiful, challenging, empowering, exhausting, life-giving experience.

When my daughter arrived, less than an hour after getting into the delivery room, looking at me with the biggest of eyes, wide awake - looking right in my soul. I'll never forget it. She knew how to find me, we knew how to work together to get her here, we are the same being, but also two beings, but also so absolutely connected.

As my body hummed with adrenaline in the recovery room, I felt this sense of awe for every woman who has ever birthed a baby.

This is how we're all here. Women are super heroes! How are we not all talking about this miracle all day every day? I am connected to this lineage, to all the ancestors who have ever given birth and those who will one day.

It was almost too much for my mind and heart to comprehend. This glimpse into understanding the magic that we all are, it feels like reverence. Like we should all be bowing to one another all day long, to the divinity that all obviously are. Each one of us is this divine spark, hidden in layers of human imperfection, here by a mix of science and grace. How could we possibly forget?

And yet, we do. We forget all the time. We forget every time we snap at one another, or cut someone off while driving, or leave a rude comment on social media. We forget when we look at each other with anything less than pure love and respect.

When we have powerful moments - glimpses that give us perspective - they help us remember.

Applications to Your Healing

THE CROWN CHAKRA HELPS YOU HEAL BY...

- Processing your relationship to religion, spirituality and faith as well as our shared humanity.

- Practicing mindfulness and meditation to study and calm the fluctuations of the mind.

- Releasing whatever you are gripping, learning to practice nonattachment.

- Seeing everything and everyone as connected, and creating enough space in your life to act from this place of remembering.

Take some time to jot down any thoughts, reactions, sensations or emotions that are present in your experience **related to your healing**. Notice anything that is coming up now that you might want to revisit later before we dive into exploring the shadow of this energetic center.

My Reflections :

Exploring the Shadow: Attachment

As I packed up my office for the last time, in the school I spent almost a decade teaching and leading, I paused to take in the moment.

It had taken months to prepare for this final goodbye. Countless meetings of sharing information with the incoming leaders, hours upon hours of sorting, recycling, donating, and decision-making.

What to keep?

What is mine?

What to leave behind?

What to let go of?

Such a practice of releasing attachment.

I remember being in meetings with one of the leaders tasked with assuming part of my role in future years, and intentionally choosing to present information in a way of "this is how I did it....what do you think?" This, to me, was evidence of growth. Previous versions of myself would have poured over the details, intent that the process be replicated exactly the same way after I was gone. But the truth is, I have no control over what they choose to do with the information. It's not mine. And evolution is all about change - sometimes quickly and sometimes incrementally.

If you've ever received art or notes from students or your own child - you know the challenge of debating what to keep and what to toss. Especially when it's made with love, the desire to hold on is so strong!

This gripping, this holding, comes from a good place. A desire to remember. But imagine for a moment this image of your hands holding onto children's art, an old mindset, your college sweatshirt, mementos from past partners. Are they full?

What are you unable to experience now because your metaphorical hands are still gripping on to the past?

As I sat in my office, walls stripped and boxes already taken to my car, I felt an overwhelming sense of peace. No tears needed to be shed. I had cried them all already. In this moment, my soul felt light. Ready. Unsure of what was coming next, but fully trusting that the right opportunities would come my way when the time was aligned. My daughter, just 12 weeks in my belly, would have time to grow, and I would have time to grow right alongside her, into this new version of myself..

The process of releasing attachment - to things, people, places, memories - is not an easy one.

When we engage in our work that we love, or when we enter into relationships with others, there is a powerful exchange of energy. We also create habits, patterns, or in yoga speak - samskaras. Grooves in the subconscious. The more we practice these patterns, the deeper they get.

At this point in my career, the identity of school leader, or educator, was central to who I was. Meet me on an airplane, that's the first thing I talk about.

When we change jobs, end a relationship, or lose someone we

love, it feels like there is a gaping hole that we might fall into. A deep groove if you will. And it's grief. It's heart-healing work. Rewiring-our-mind work.

It's remembering that we are not our jobs, our roles in our family, or other identities. Those are aspects of who we are, but they are not us. Who we are at our core is so much more than that, and also so much simpler than that. *I'm a soul on a journey...who was an assistant principal for a while.*

Imagine if you - and I - were able to set aside the labels we give ourselves. Hold our hands wide open, ready to receive and give away anything that came through. Finances, a home, job title, success, personality quirks. What if we remembered that it all is temporary?

How much more would we be able to experience fully if we were willing to also let it go afterward?

In the summer after leaving my school, I felt this samskara being rewritten as I fumbled over my words introducing myself to others in prenatal yoga class. It felt awkward and vulnerable to be in this empty place between such purposeful work, and an unknown future.

I experimented with keeping it simple. "I'm Jess...I'm practicing being really present in my pregnancy, which some days is beautiful and easy, and some days incredibly hard."

It felt good to be honest. It felt good to be seen and received as another soul in the room, riding waves of emotion, practicing being in my body. And letting that be enough.

This shadow of attachment creeps up everywhere. From the mundane - *why am I unable to give away this sweater I haven't worn in a decade?* - to the existential - *why is it so hard to separate my worth from my productivity?*

And so we practice.

We notice our thoughts, breathe deeply, and release our attachments when we can.

"We notice the thoughts, breathe deeply, and release our attachments when we can."

Exploring this chakra is an opportunity to get curious around your relationship to your **individual and our collective wholeness.** Are you able to connect with something that is bigger than your own experience? What conditions support your ability to experience peace, trust, and non-attachment?

My Reflections :

All of this information influences how you know yourself as a leader.

Applications to Your Leadership

THE CROWN CHAKRA HELPS YOU LEAD BY...
• Conceptualizing the larger picture as you move through daily work.
• Remembering the individual as well as the collective in decisions, designs, and experiences.
• Observing thought loops and patterns, and using introspective practices to guide your leadership, specifically allowing for insight and wisdom to come through.
• Bringing a "human first approach" to your work by creating moments of connection between people in meetings, workshops and informal settings.

On the adjacent page, take some time to jot down any thoughts, reactions, sensations or emotions that are present in your experience **related to your leadership.** Note any ideas, connections or musings you want to remember before we think about specific moments where you and I both have chosen to Lead with Connection.

My Reflections :

A Moment I Decided to Lead with Connection

One fall weekend when Gabby was still in preschool, we took an extra day for a quick trip up the coast. Camping and encouraging adventure is one of my favorite ways to be a leader in our family.

As always, nature delivered.

Contemplating the vastness of the universe with Jason once Gabby was snoozing was a total highlight for me. We craned our necks to look up at the stars, we checked out our shadows being cast by the brightness of the moon, and we talked about big things - the sustainability of our planet, our time here and how it makes us want to make the most of it.

We wondered about the possibility of other life; what it might look like, being humbled by the fact that our sun is just one of so many stars.

We hugged big trees and listened to the wisdom that they have to share. The ancient coastal redwoods never cease to amaze me. Their sheer size, the journeys that they've been through, how they have intertwined with one another, or been hollowed out through the storms that life brings.

We gazed at the roots, exposed from their fall, which is always an invitation to check in with our own. To more firmly plant ourselves in the here and now.

We visited the ocean, strained to see it through the fog, and then smiled as the light revealed the blues and greens and teals, and the water sparkled with sunlight. We tasted Olallieberries, growing naturally by the sea cliffs.

Just slow down.

This whole trip was less than 48 hours, yet I felt so refreshed when we got home. (Don't let me fool you, sleeping in a tent with an almost five-year-old is not the best night of sleep of my life, but my soul was refreshed.)

I remember that most of what we think as urgent, can actually wait a beat. That the intensity of a moment will inevitably pass. In short, I'm reminded to hold things lightly. This is my consistent message when I tune into nature.

Hold things lightly.

The whispers I receive from nature - *that we are all connected to each other, to everything here and now, and all that came before and is still yet to come* - they remind me that each moment is so beautiful and unique and totally special, and it's gone before we realize it. It's a constant invitation to slow things down, make our moments matter, and hold all of it with open palms so we can keep the perspective of how this experience is connected to everything else.

Contemplation helps us see the connection to all humanity hidden in the heartache we inevitably experience throughout our lives.

We all experience loss. We all experience joy.

The new growth is only made possible when the old (tree, mindset, ways of being) dies away. It helps us see the tenderness revealed through shedding old armor and the compassion gained from being in a tough situation. When we lead from this place of connection, we see everything with a wiser perspective.

One of Your Stories

- What do you want to say about your relationship to spirituality and recognizing our shared humanity and how it impacts you as a leader in your life now?

- Write a story about connection. Who is there? Where are you? What does it feel like?

- Think of a time you felt balanced in this seventh chakra or aspect of yourself, when you felt deeply connected to all living things and/or spirit.

- Think of a time you healed something related to letting go. Is there a story about attachment that wants to be told? Surrender as you write this story.

IT'S ALL CONNECTED

Embodiment Practices

The meditation and yoga can be practiced separately, or in either order. Experiment and see what feels most supportive in quieting the mind.

Meditation Script
(tap into peace and wisdom)

As you prepare for this meditation, find a comfortable seated or reclined position. Take a few breaths to settle the body, and get as present as you can.

In this practice, we'll engage in a strategy called "noting" where as you notice thoughts arising, you label them and allow them to then float on by.

Some common patterns for thoughts are "planning" "analyzing" "time traveling" "daydreaming" "worrying" or whatever feels relevant to the thoughts that emerge for you.

If you have access to an audio form that occasionally chimes the singing bowls, use this as a reminder to return to the practice.

Having thoughts emerge is not "doing it wrong", it's part of the practice of understanding the patterns in our mind. Returning to the breath is the practice. Every time you remember and return, you are strengthening the groove for returning to the present moment.

- - - *(give silence to practice)* - - -

Begin to deepen your breath. Invite small movements into fingers and toes, circle ankles and wrists. Reach arms and legs in opposite directions and take a big stretch, maybe a sigh. Find your way up to a seat, grab your journal and write down any reflections from your practice.

My Reflections :

How to practice

Throughout this meditative flow, use your awareness to be deeply present in the poses to help embody the thought element. Feel the crown of the head and notice the mind in each pose.

Leading with Connection is all about surrender, so consider how you could release attachment to certain outcomes in each posture. Allow this particular sequence to be transformative.

Warm up

1 MOUNTAIN UPWARD SALUTE

2 FORWARD FOLD

3 HALFWAY LIFT

4 PLANK

REPEAT 5X

5 DOWNWARD FACING DOG

6 HALFWAY LIFT

7 FORWARD FOLD

8 MOUNTAIN ANJALI MUDRA

Flows

1A HIGH LUNGE

1B WARRIOR THREE

1C STANDING SPLITS

1D PYRAMID

RESET. REPEAT.

2A WARRIOR TWO

2B STANDING WIDE LEG BACKBEND

2C STANDING WIDE LEG FORWARD FOLD W/ BIND

2D WIDE LEGGED FOLD W/ TWIST

RESET. REPEAT.

3A CHILD'S POSE W/ PRAYER HANDS

3B DOLPHIN

option for...

3C TRIPOD HEADSTAND

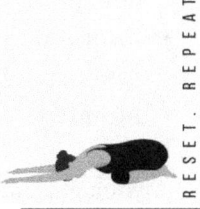

3D CHILD'S POSE

RESET. REPEAT.

4A LOCUST W/ ARMS OVERHEAD

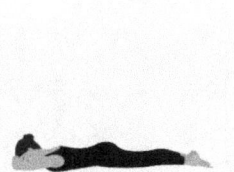

4B CROCODILE

4C RABBIT

4D SEATED FORWARD FOLD

RESET. REPEAT.

Cool Down

1 SEATED TWIST

2 COW FACE

-or-

3 EASY SEAT OR LOTUS

-or-

4 SEATED MEDITATION OR REST

how to engage with the theme of

CONNECTION

body

- Hydrate well and nourish your brain.
- Incorporate rest and space in your day.
- Include inversions and rest (savasana) at the end of your yoga practice.
- Follow your body's natural cycles and rhythms.
- Notice the relationship between movement/stillness and the quality of your thoughts.

mind

- Practice extended meditation - find space between the thoughts.
- Engage in a technology detox.
- Review past journals to reflect on the nature of change and extract wisdom.
- Meditate on your mantra or affirmation.
- Engage in therapy or coaching to unearth subconscious beliefs.

soul

- Connect with nature (e.g. stars, mountains, water).
- Do a candle-gazing meditation practice.
- Spend time with people who your soul deeply connects with.
- Explore spiritual practices that speak to you.
- Practice Loving-Kindness meditation to offer peace to all beings everywhere.

work

- Mentor or seek mentorship.
- Weave reflective practices into your schedule.
- Offer moments for human connection and healing for self and others at work.
- Call on past wisdom to support in challenging moments.
- Mind map, brainstorm, and engage in thought exercises to consider all ideas.

Leading
with
CONNECTION
means...

- Embodying the thought element to understand that you are not your mind, but you are in partnership with it.
- Tuning into the wisdom of nature and our shared humanity.
- Having a spiritual practice that both grounds and inspires you.
- Creating sacred pauses in your day that allow you to remember the larger picture.
- Knowing there is a thread of connection between everything past, present and future.
- Experiencing peace in between your thoughts.

PROMPTS FOR FURTHER REFLECTION

1. Wisdom is gained when we transform our experiences then connect and apply what we learned in a new context. What piece of wisdom would you offer a younger version of yourself?

2. Look at your life as it is now. What connections can you make between your purpose, your daily actions, and the larger impact you're having on the world around you?

3. When you let yourself zoom out and take a wide perspective on your week, what wisdom do you remember about your life and your leadership?

4. Consider how moving your body or sitting in stillness impacted your connection to your leadership this week.

My Reflections : _____

_____

_____

_____

_____

_____

_____

_____

_____

_____

_____

_____

_____

_____

_____

_____

_____

_____

_____

_____

_____

IT'S ALL CONNECTED

C O N N E C T I O N

In Summary...

- Leading with Connection correlates to the crown chakra.

- Exploring, embodying and spending time observing the thought element can deepen your connection to this theme.

- Learning about, healing and loving your relationship with your mind, your connectedness with everything and everyone around you as well as the planet is where all the work of previous themes come together. Notice all the opportunities for healing here.

- Exploring your connections, your attachments and your thoughts is deep and ongoing work. Connect with your community as you go.

Leadership Integration: "I Evolve"

"Wholeness is not achieved by cutting off a portion of one's being, but by integration of the contraries."

~Carl Jung

Where We Conclude

If you're here and you've worked your way through these themes, chapters, and practices, I'm curious if this is a question that you're wondering: "Now what?"

It's almost always the question at the end of a learning experience.

Now what?

What will I choose do with this information?

If you have been integrating as you go, you might not have that question because you've been asking it all along.

If we revisit the analogy of a yoga practice, we have arrived at savasana, rest. If we fully translate savasana, it's more than rest, it translates to "corpse pose". It is the symbolic ending or death.

Things are dying all the time - old mindsets, the leaves on the trees, the battery on your phone - it's part of the cycle.

So maybe a better question to ask is, "What part of my identity, my ways of being, or my mindset no longer belong here? What needs to die, or be released, in order to create space for new life to emerge?"

Maybe you're ready to release identifying as a perfectionist or workaholic. Or maybe you're ready to shed the label as someone who is too shy to lead. Or perhaps it's time to let go of the old belief that you don't deserve as much happiness as the people you support.

In the space created by letting that old identity melt away, maybe you can now invite in more rest, more softness, more vulnerability, more space, more boldness, more love, more confidence.

Because it's cyclical work, sometimes it's hard to know how exactly this integration happens.

Did I crowd out the belief that my worth is dependent on my productivity because I incorporated more space and more rest?

Maybe.

Did small behaviors and actions and phrases one at a time dry up like a leaf in the fall, and eventually crumple and make their way down to the earth? So subtle, if I'm not watching I'll miss it, but then one day I look up and the tree is totally different.

Maybe.

In my own life, when I look around, I see there's so much more space. So many things have changed - the way I earn money for my family, the way I introduce myself when I meet someone new, my ability to pause mid-project and put it down for a bit, the way I believe I deserve to rest.

To me, this is what integration looks like, *subtle shifts accumulated over time.*

Like the way a child grows - microscopic measurement by microscopic measurement, day after day after day. Until all of a sudden, it's hard to understand how this walking and talking five year old once fit inside my body.

When we take this zoomed out perspective, growth is easy to see.

Integrating Our Learning Matters

Here's my invitation to you right now. Zoom out. Pause and let your mind wander back to when you first picked up this book.

- What has changed for you?
- How have you changed?
- What has been left behind and no longer represents what you think, believe or do?
- What has been integrated and is now just part of who you are?

My Reflections :

At the end of savasana, when I'm guiding class, I'll say "begin to deepen your breath". That sound of collective awakening...it's one of my favorite moments in the whole practice.

From the depths of rest, we begin to re-emerge, slightly different from when we began. As we invite gentle movement back into the body, reconnecting the mind, body and spirit, it's an opportunity to pause and notice - what's shifted? What has integrated?

Returning to the same seat we began in, where we set our intentions, I always invite the class to bring hands over the heart, and take a moment to show ourselves some gratitude and feel the effects of your practice.

That's where we are right now - collective awakening, meeting ourselves in this new moment with gratitude and awareness.

I'd love for you to do the same, right here and right now, place both hands over your heart. Show yourself some gratitude and feel the effects of your practice. This practice, this journey of working through these themes.

Then we offer it out. We pray that the benefits of our practice bring more peace to ourselves, to each other, *to all beings everywhere.*

So let's take this and get practical.

How does integration look on a day-to-day level as a leader and as you continue on your healing journey?

In terms of leadership, I think of integration as regularly providing a pause to reflect for yourself, and for those you serve.

This could be a daily journaling practice. A commitment to write down three learnings at the end of the day. Consider all the ways you have worked through and engaged in learning over the course of the book. Notice what practices, modalities, and exercises were most organically integrated into your life *already*. Or think about which ones were especially meaningful that you would like to bring back into a regular rotation moving forward.

Here's the beautiful thing - you can choose your cadence - daily, weekly, monthly, quarterly, yearly. Whether you're aspiring to be a better leader for yourself, for a team, or for your family, it's all valuable.

It can be simple. The important part is to include practices and moments that allow for the integration to occur.

Being a Leader in My Own Life

- What did I learn about myself?
- What did I learn about my leadership?
- What did I learn about my community and what they need?
- What's working?
- What could use an adjustment?

Being a Leader of a Team

- What are we collectively learning about ourselves, each other and our work and our impact?
- What strengths are we noticing in one another that lift up our team?
- What are the top three insights you have from this learning experience?

Being a Leader in My Family

- What are we learning about how we show up for one another?
- What's working for our family?
- What needs adjusting?
- What routines need shifting as we individually and collectively learn and grow?

I invite you to take a moment and jot down some thoughts about what integration practices you might want to carry forward.

My Reflections :

One of My Stories

Nature helps me integrate. And thank goodness for that, because we live in a tree house.

Not literally, but it feels like one. Our home seems to have more windows than walls, and when you look out, it's mostly green. You could tell yourself that you were a squirrel and it would feel true at times. We've been in this house for a couple years, and it's one of the best decisions we've ever made.

I have the opportunity to walk up a big hill each morning and step on a trail that winds through the California Redwoods. Some mornings are foggy, others the light streams through the trees. Some seasons are muddy and I return home with shoes that I should really just leave outside. Some mornings it's just me and the birds, and others I nod and wave to my trail friends who I see frequently but know nothing about, not even their name.

Choosing to visit this trail more days than not is a way I integrate what I'm learning.

I think more clearly here. I breathe more deeply. I've cried and hugged these trees. I've danced. I've had brilliant ideas. I've sat on the bench and meditated. I've watched seasons change. I've forgiven myself. I've forgiven others. I've remembered.

I know that I am a more present mother, partner, coach, yoga teacher, daughter, sister, friend and fellow human because I actively choose to spend time in nature each day. Nature helps me remember our connection, which supports my ability to show up with love. The type of love that sees the best in people - "I see your soul" type love.

And then I forget, because I'm a human. And so I go again. Or I sit quietly and breathe until I remember. Or I write until I remember. Or I practice yoga and clear some energy until I remember.

It takes discipline. It takes realistic self-compassion. I know that I will forget, and I love myself anyway. I trust that the tools I have will help me remember, and so I schedule them in. I know that a cold rainy run on my trail is harder to do, but I do it anyway. Because it helps me stay in service - to myself, to my family, to you.

Much of this book has been written on this trail. Me, speaking into my phone. Remembering.

The classic Sanskrit mantra Lokah Samastah Sukhino Bhavantu translates to *"May all beings everywhere be happy and free, and may the thoughts, words, and actions of my own life contribute in some way to that happiness and to that freedom for all."*

To me, this is the point of it all. That our thoughts, words and actions are connected to the collective. When we act consciously, we can bring more healing, more peace into the world - it creates ripple effects.

This small act of peace and love, it matters. This offering of purposeful creativity, it matters. This act of self-love and healing, it matters. When I take time to heal myself, so I can show up more fully to heal others, it matters.

Integrating is about continually seeking wholeness - within ourselves and between all things.

Embodiment Practices

The meditation and yoga can be practiced separately, or in either order. Experiment and see what feels most supportive in relaxing into a sense of awe and gratitude.

Meditation Script
(tap into deep rest and appreciation)

Find a comfortable place for your body. Fully relax into your seated or laying down position. Allow the hands to land wherever is most comfortable. Breathe.

Invite in several rounds of deep breath, feeling the lungs and belly expand and contract. Let it be intentional, but full of ease.

Then begin to scan through the body, noticing it as if for the first time. When you reach each new part of the body, give it your full attention - noticing how it may have changed over time. Did it always feel this way? What is new and fresh and wonderful about how your feet feel today? Or your heart? Or your eyes?

Show some deep love and appreciation to each part of your body as you visit it with your awareness, thanking it for being on this journey with you.

Take your time.

When you are complete, end with gratitude. Thank you, thank you, thank you.

You can invite in some deeper breaths, and gentle movements. Eventually returning to a seated position. Grab your journal and reflect on how you feel.

LEADERSHIP INTEGRATION
Yoga Sequence

How to Practice

In this restorative sequence, let yourself deeply relax. These poses are meant to be held for longer amounts of time. As you set yourself up in each shape, become as comfortable as you can, so there is as little effort as possible.

Close the eyes, and let yourself rest on purpose. That is the best way to receive the benefits of these postures and allow the nervous system to switch into "rest and digest", the parasympathetic state.

Restorative Yoga Sequence

4 minutes here...

CONSTRUCTIVE REST

A NOTE ABOUT THE POSE:
This opening pose is meant to help you arrive. Options include:
- Laying the spine over a bolster
- Placing one block under the head, and one under the shoulder blades

4 minutes on each side...

SUPINE TWIST-- R AND L

A NOTE ABOUT THE POSE:
Find a version of a twist where you can soften and release any effort. Prioritize keeping your shoulders on the mat. It's not about how deep you can twist, more about letting your body relax into the shape.

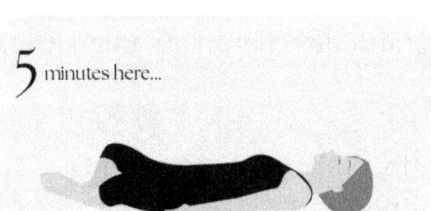

5 minutes here...

SUPINE BUTTERFLY

A NOTE ABOUT THE POSE:
Options include:
- Arms by your sides
- One hand over your heart, and the other over your belly
- Blocks underneath the knees to lessen strain in the groin

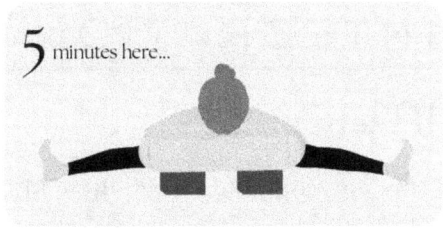

5 minutes here...

SEATED WIDE LEG FORWARD FOLD W/ BOLSTER

A NOTE ABOUT THE POSE :

The intention here is to turn inward, let the mind rest, and invite the body to soften.

Position your legs where you feel a gentle opening, but no strain.

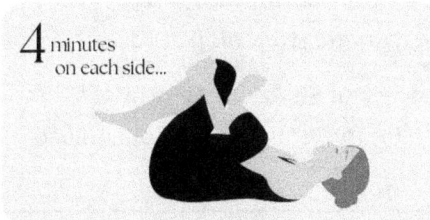

4 minutes on each side...

REVERSE PIGEON (ON EACH SIDE)

A NOTE ABOUT THE POSE :

Prioritize keeping the natural curves of your spine on the mat: the back of the head, the upper spine, and the tailbone. Do your best to maintain ease everywhere else.

6 minutes here...

LEGS UP THE WALL

A NOTE ABOUT THE POSE :

Sliding your body up against a literal wall is such a nice way to enjoy the benefits of this pose and release. Or, extend the legs up wherever you are. You can slide a block under your sacrum for a little extra elevation.

10 minutes here...

SAVASANA- ENJOY THE EXTENDED REST

A NOTE ABOUT THE POSE :

Deeply rest here. Options include:
* Adding a bolster or blanket under your knees
* Covering yourself with a blanket or layers to keep warm
* Wearing an eye mask

LEADERSHIP INTEGRATION

In Summary...

- Integration is when we bring our new learnings and embed them into our ways of being.

- Integration is always happening, but can be done intentionally in our professional and personal lives to deepen personal growth.

- Journaling, meditation, rest, verbally processing with others or creating new habits are all ways we can integrate on purpose.

- If you have taken notes, written stories, or shared with others over the course of this book, you have been integrating all along. Pause and notice how you have evolved.

PROMPTS FOR FURTHER REFLECTION

I intentionally repeated the same prompts from the chapter on Leadership Intentions so you could take note of your own growth!

1. How are you engaging with your leadership intention now? How has it shifted since beginning this book? Describe a moment where you spent a little extra time with your intention recently and what the result was.

2. If your best friend were to describe you as a leader, what words would they use? How does it feel to see yourself as a leader through their eyes? How has this changed from all the way back in the beginning?

3. What is something that a past version of you would be so excited about/proud of?

4. Consider how moving your body or sitting in stillness impacted your connection to your leadership.

My Reflections : _____

_____

_____

_____

_____

_____

_____

_____

_____

_____

_____

_____

_____

_____

_____

_____

_____

_____

_____

_____

_____

IT'S ALL CONNECTED

IT'S ALL CONNECTED

Final Prayer

The journey of integration brings us alllll the way back to the beginning. When we revisit the newest, most evolved version of ourselves, we have the opportunity to begin again. To set a new intention. With each breath, we can do that.

And when we set that new intention, we're always invited to reconnect with our purpose, which we know is grounded in love and service. We root ourselves in this fresh moment, with all the wisdom we have now, and we move through.

How can you bring creativity and energy to this revised purpose? What would it feel like to confidently bring this purpose to light? How can you breathe more love and space into it and then speak it out in the world? Can you see this vision - both in your deepest inner wisdom and as it connects to the larger spiritual picture?

It's big work.

It's also *connected* work.

I hope that you revisit this book. That when the next growth edge appears in your life, and we both know it will, you start at the beginning. It might be when you change careers. Or you move to a new city. Or a relationship ends, or one begins. If you're a parent, it could be as your child grows and who you are shifts. Your parents might be aging and who takes care of who has suddenly swapped. The identity changes we experience as our familial responsibilities adjust are big ones.

Regardless of the catalyst, know that this book is here for you. You can pick it back up and begin again.

You can set your intentions, ground in your purpose and tell new stories. Your foundation will in some ways be the same, but at each new stage of life, you'll have new wisdom, new perspective, and different things matter most.

I truly hope that the questions, the exercises, and the story prompts inspire deeper reflections when you find yourself in a new moment of change and evolution. That it brings you into a new level of wholeness as you integrate the new experiences.

I wish you many blessings as you continue on this path.

I'll be doing this work right alongside you.

Learning, growing and healing.

May you evolve *with ease.*

Acknowledgements

Jason, my loving husband. Back when I finished my first yoga teacher training, I wrote you a letter. It was an emotional experience and I felt so loved and seen by you throughout. I would come home and try to put into words moments and exercises that are hard to describe without being there. You would listen for hours - not needing to have experienced it yourself to love me through it. In that letter to you, I said I was so grateful that you loved the future version of me. That I knew you did, without a doubt. That whatever changes life brought our way, I knew at my very core that you already loved that version of me, probably more than I even did. Many things have changed in our lives since that letter, but your constancy and steadiness has not. Thank you for your endless listening, your research skills, your commitment to figuring it out, whatever it is. For your love, support, and your belief in me. I love you.

Mom, thank you for decades of love and support, for bringing me into the world, for being my biggest cheerleader and for reading every single word of this book with a fine tooth comb. Your words of encouragement mean so much to me. Thank you for the gift of being witnessed and for your attention to the details. Your eye for consistency initiated so many impactful changes. The book is so much better for having passed through your capable hands. I love you so much.

Jenna, my designer and editor and friend of so many years, I literally could not have put this book together without you. Your joy in the design, your creative eye, and your willingness to jump in headfirst to this project with me is appreciated more than you'll ever know. Thank you for bringing this book to life one page at a time with so much care. So much love to you!

To the women in It's All Connected, our yearlong journey. Oh my goodness, I love you. Thank you for showing up month after month as this book unfolded. For your vulnerability, your encouragement, your desire for community and your generous love. We did it. I am endlessly grateful for your presence throughout this process.

To all my teachers, thank you for your wisdom. In here, I include my formal teachers, and those who imparted wisdom in passing. When we're paying attention, there are teachers everywhere. For those who I have studied under, I am so lucky to have been in the right place at the right time to learn from you. That our paths crossed when they did. Know that I am forever changed as a result. The impact you made is felt and moving through me onto others.

To my siblings, my extended family, my chosen family - friends from childhood through adulthood, I'm so grateful for the large and small ways our lives have overlapped, influenced, inspired, challenged and changed us. When I think about my roots - where I belong - this is you. Thank you.

To Gabrielle. Gabby. My sweetest girl. Thank you for being here. For choosing me. For being excited with and for me as I wrote this book. For showing up in my life when and how you did, and for the million tiny moments you share your love. From butterfly kisses to silly dances to beach adventures to waking me up each morning, I hope you continue to grow and thrive and encourage everyone around you to do the same. Mama loves you to the moon and back.

Endnotes

◆ INTRODUCTION

1. Corn, S. (2020). *Revolution of the Soul: Awaken to love through raw truth, radical healing, and conscious action* (p. 50-54). Sounds True.
2. Corn, S. (2020). *Revolution of the Soul: Awaken to love through raw truth, radical healing, and conscious action* (p. 105). Sounds True.
3. Bachman, N. (2011). *The Path of the Yoga Sutras a practical guide to the core of yoga* (p. 185). Sounds True.
4. Adele, D. (2009). *The Yamas & Niyamas: Exploring yoga's ethical practice.* On-Word Bound Books.

◆ LEAD WITH PURPOSE

5. Jimenez, M. P., DeVille, N. V., Elliott, E. G., Schiff, J. E., Wilt, G. E., Hart, J. E., & James, P. (2021). Associations between nature exposure and health: A review of the evidence. International Journal of Environmental Research and Public Health, 18(9), 4790. https://doi.org/10.3390/ijerph18094790
6. van der Kolk, B. A. (2014). *The Body Keeps The Score: Brain, Mind, and Body in the Healing of Trauma.* Viking.

◆ Lead with Creativity

7. Brown, B. (2021) *Atlas of the Heart*. Random House.
8. United States Geological Survey. (n.d.). How much water is there on Earth? https://www.usgs.gov/special-topics/water-science school/science/how-much-water-there-earth
9. Scripps Health. (2021, July 7). The surprising health benefits of blue spaces. https://www.scripps.org/news_items/7657-the-surprising-health-benefits-of-blue-space

◆ Lead with Confidence

10. California College of Ayurveda. (n.d.). Five elements: Fire in Ayurveda. National Institutes of Health. (2021, May). Embodied trauma & somatic approaches. National Center for Biotechnology Information. https://pmc.ncbi.nlm.nih.gov/articles/PMC8125471/
11. Plumb, L. (2021). *Ayurveda Cooking for Beginners: An Ayurvedic cookbook to balance & heal.* New World Library.

◆ Lead with Love

12. Grow Billion Trees. (n.d.). How trees benefit humans. https://growbilliontrees.com/blogs/knowledge/how-trees-benefits-humans
13. Werner, D. (2016). *The Illuminated Breath*. (pg. 93) New World Library.

◆ Lead with Truth

14. Yale Baby School. (n.d.). Does my baby recognize me? https://babyschool.yale.edu/does-my-baby-recognize-me/
15. Judith, A. (2004). *The Wheels of Life: A user's guide to the chakra system* (pp. 255–257). Llewellyn Publications.

◆ Lead with Intuition

16. Sleep Foundation. (n.d.). Blue light and sleep. https://www.sleepfoundation.org/bedroom-environment/blue-light
17. Corn, S. (2020). *Revolution of the Soul: Awaken to love through raw truth, radical healing, and conscious action*(p. 159). Sounds True.

◆ Lead with Connection

18. Singer, M. A. (2007). *The untethered soul: The journey beyond yourself* (p. 42). New Harbinger Publications.
19. Aguilar, E. (2018). *Onward: Cultivating emotional resilience in educators* (p. 71). Jossey-Bass.
20. American Psychological Association. (2012, July/August). *The social self: Who we are and how we connect.* https://www.apa.org/monitor/2012/07-08/ce-corner

References

- Adele, D. (2009). *The Yamas & Niyamas: Exploring yoga's ethical practice.* On-Word Bound Books.
- Aguilar, E. (2020). Coaching for equity: Conversations that change practice (1st ed.). Jossey-Bass.
- Aguilar, E. (2018). *Onward: Cultivating emotional resilience in educators.* Jossey-Bass.
- American Forests. (n.d.). People and trees: An intimate connection. https://www.americanforests.org/article/people-and-trees-an-intimate-connection/
- American Psychological Association. (2012, July/August). The social self: Who we are and how we connect. https://www.apa.org/monitor/2012/07-08/ce-corner
- Arhanta Yoga. (n.d.). 7 chakras: Introduction to the energy centers & their effect. https://www.arhantayoga.org/blog/7-chakras-introduction-energy-centers-effect/
- Bachman, N. (2011). *The Path of the Yoga Sutras a practical guide to the core of yoga* (p. 185). Sounds True.
- Brown, B. (2021)Atlas of the Heart. Random House.
- California College of Ayurveda. (n.d.). Five elements: Fire in Ayurveda. National Institutes of Health. https://pmc.ncbi.nlm.nih.gov/articles/PMC8125471/
- Chakras.info. (n.d.). Chakra colors. https://www.chakras.info/chakra-colors/
- Clara Roberts-Oss. (n.d.). Ajna chakra: Trust your intuition. https://www.clararobertsoss.com/ajna-chakra-trust-your-intuition/
- Corn, S. (2020). *Revolution of the soul: Awaken to love through raw truth, radical healing, and conscious action.* Sounds True.
- Grow Billion Trees. (n.d.). How trees benefit humans. https://growbilliontrees.com/blogs/knowledge/how-trees-benefits-humans
- Healthline. (2019, December 18). 7 chakras: What they mean and how to unblock them. https://www.healthline.com/health/fitness-exercise/7-chakras#Chakra-101
- Healthline. (2021, September 23). Left brain vs. right brain: What's the difference? https://www.healthline.com/health/left-brain-vs-right-brain#left-brain-vs-right-brain-myth

References (cont.)

- Jimenez, M. P., DeVille, N. V., Elliott, E. G., Schiff, J. E., Wilt, G. E., Hart, J. E., & James, P. (2021). Associations between nature exposure and health: A review of the evidence. International Journal of Environmental Research and Public Health, 18(9), 4790. https://doi.org/10.3390/ijerph18094790
- Judith, A. (2004). The wheels of life: A user's guide to the chakra system. Llewellyn Publications.
- Medical News Today. (2023, February 27). What percentage of the human body is water? https://www.medicalnewstoday.com/articles/what-percentage-of-the-human-body-is-water
- Mindbodygreen. (n.d.). 7 chakra colors and what they mean. https://www.mindbodygreen.com/articles/7-chakra-colors-what-they-mean-and-why-they-matter
- Mindbodygreen. (n.d.). 7 chakras for beginners. https://www.mindbodygreen.com/articles/7-chakras-for-beginners
- Plumb, L. (2021). *Ayurveda cooking for beginners: An Ayurvedic cookbook to balance & heal.* New World Library.
- Scripps Health. (2021, July 7). The surprising health benefits of blue spaces. https://www.scripps.org/news_items/7657-the-surprising-health-benefits-of-blue-space
- Singer, M. A. (2007). *The untethered soul: The journey beyond yourself.* New Harbinger Publications.
- Sleep Foundation. (n.d.). Blue light and sleep. https://www.sleepfoundation.org/bedroom-environment/blue-light
- United States Geological Survey. (n.d.). How much water is there on Earth? https://www.usgs.gov/special-topics/water-science-school/science/how-much-water-there-earth
- van der Kolk, B. A. (2014). *The Body Keeps The Score: Brain, mind, and body in the healing of trauma.* Viking.
- Werner, D. (2016). *The illuminated breath.* New World Library.
- WestEd. (n.d.). Mindfulness-based practices for schools. https://www.wested.org/resources/mindfulness-based-practices-for-schools/
- Yale Baby School. (n.d.). Does my baby recognize me? https://babyschool.yale.edu/does-my-baby-recognize-me/

About the Author

Jessica Boots is a writer, transformational leadership coach, yoga teacher (E-RYT 500, RPYT) and mama who supports introspective, heart-led humans in evolving their leadership from the inside out. As the founder of Lead and Be Well, she blends mindfulness, wellness, and professional growth to help others show up with authenticity and purpose. A lifelong question-asker, Jess brings her background in education, yoga, and personal transformation to create work that's both reflective and deeply practical.

Learn more at www.leadandbewell.com
Follow Jess on social media 🅞 @leadandbewell

About the Designer

Jenna Zakrajsek has spent her career championing literacy, guiding teachers, and creating spaces where all readers can thrive. With a passion for foundational reading skills and a newfound, growing love for design, she gravitates toward work that honors both function and feeling—where creativity serves a deeper purpose. Jenna brings her background in teaching, leadership, and creativity to *It's All Connected*—her very first design project—with immense gratitude and joy.

Praise for *It's All Connected*

"If you're searching for a guide on the journey to connect your leadership potential to your own unique energy centers- look no further! Jessica seamlessly integrates the interconnectedness of leadership and the seven chakras - teaching us how to tap into our own abilities and truths so we can become the best mothers, partners, friends and individuals we are capable of being. You will feel validated and empowered as you read this book, almost as if Jessica were right in front of you, holding space for a private journey of healing."
~Kayla McCaffrey,
Mama of 4, VP of Operations and Chief Advocate at Paper for Water

"It is an honor to celebrate my friend, the visionary behind Lead and Be Well, whose work stands at the intersection of heart-centered leadership and holistic wellness. With grace, wisdom, and lived experience, she reminds us through *It's All Connected* that the most powerful leaders are those who lead from within. This book is both a guide and a gift—inviting us to align our values, actions, and well-being for lasting impact."
~Kris Naranjo,
Head of People and Operations at Oakland Promise

"Wise and empowering, with teachings and practices to support your learning and growth. Jessica encourages you on your journey of self discovery and inspires you to fully embrace life with joy while remaining connected to your values."
~Amy Landuyt
Analyst

"*It's All Connected* is a beautiful journey of self-discovery, learning, and growth. Jess offers us tangible ways to bring the wisdom of the chakras into our leadership and daily lives. It's one thing to learn about these ideas, but it's another to embody them. This book gives us the *how*."
~Kelsey Lettko
Integrative Hypnotherapist

342

Praise for *It's All Connected*

"Jess's book, *It's All Connected*, is a powerful invitation to pause, reflect, and lead from within, blending intuition with grounded leadership. Her insights remind me that true wisdom comes from balancing data and decisions with the quiet knowing of the heart and mind. Through her guidance, I am learning to embrace clarity, compassion, and courage in my leadership journey, trusting that the best version of myself already resides within."
~Kim Parks-Brazil,
Director of Teaching and Learning

"Each chapter is full of opportunities to think deeper, heal, and grow as a leader and an individual. Jess engages us with strong insights and teachings, which allow us to consider new ideas and perspectives. As you connect with this book, you develop a deeper connection with yourself and your journey."
~Elizabeth Marks
Kindergarten Teacher

"This life-changing book was a true joy to read! It's conversational tone drew me in from the first chapter onward. I truly enjoyed internalizing her messages through suggested exercises, journaling, prompts, and yoga sequences. You won't be able to put this down and will revisit it year after year as you start new chapters of your life."
~Sharon Goeman,
Senior Manager (retired)

"From *It's All Connected* I have gained so many practical strategies to help me feel more aligned with my values, and I really appreciate the choose-your-own-adventure aspect where there's something for everyone and I can pick strategies that feel right to me in whatever season I'm in."
~Darina Neal,
Workforce Health Consultant

www.ingramcontent.com/pod-product-compliance
Lightning Source LLC
Chambersburg PA
CBHW061553120626
46550CB00004B/1478